Non-League
Supporters'
Guide
& Yearbook
2010

EDITOR
John Robinson

Eighteenth Edition

For details of our range of over 1,500 books and 300 DVDs, visit our web site or contact us using the information shown below.

British Library Cataloguing in Publication Data
A catalogue record for this book is available from the British Library

ISBN: 978-1-86223-183-2

Manufactured in the UK by LPPS Ltd, Wellingborough, NN8 3PJ

FOREWORD

Our thanks go to the numerous club officials who have aided us in the compilation of information contained in this guide and also to Michael Robinson (page layouts), Bob Budd (cover artwork) and Tony Brown (Cup Statistics – www.soccerdata.com) for the part they have played.

Where we use the term 'Child' for concessionary prices, this is often also the price charged to Senior Citizens. Readers should also note that matchday admission prices should increase in December 2009 when the proposed VAT increase back up to 17.5% comes into force.

Following the recent demise of Setanta Sports, many of the Step 1 & 2 clubs are facing considerable financial difficulties and it is even possible that the future of some may be jeopardy.

However, we are only able to present the position as it stands when we go to press and we, as always, have to advise our readers that the fixtures shown in this guide may alter to reflect any changes of this nature.

Finally, we would like to wish our readers a safe and happy spectating season.

John Robinson
EDITOR

CONTENTS

The Football Conference Blue Square Premier Clubs & Information 5-29

The Football Conference Blue Square North Clubs & Information 30-52

The Football Conference Blue Square South Clubs & Information 53-75

2008/2009 Statistics for the Nationwide Conference National 76

2008/2009 Statistics for the Nationwide Conference North 77

2008/2009 Statistics for the Nationwide Conference South 78

2008/2009 Statistics for the Unibond Premier Division 79

2008/2009 Stats. for the Southern Premier League – Premier Division 80

2008/2009 Statistics for the Isthmian Premier Division 81

2008/2009 F.A. Trophy Results 82-86

2008/2009 F.A. Vase Results 87-91

2009/2010 Season Fixtures for the Football Conference 92-94

Advertisement: Non-League Football Tables books 95

Advertisement: The Supporters' Guide Series 96

THE FOOTBALL CONFERENCE BLUE SQUARE NATIONAL

Address   Third Floor, Wellington House, 31-34 Waterloo Street, Birmingham   B2 5TJ

Phone (0121) 214-1950

Web site   www.footballconference.co.uk

Clubs for the 2009/2010 Season

AFC Wimbledon .... Page 6
Altrincham FC .... Page 7
Barrow FC .... Page 8
Cambridge United FC .... Page 9
Chester City FC .... Page 10
Crawley Town FC .... Page 11
Eastbourne Borough FC .... Page 12
Ebbsfleet United FC .... Page 13
Forest Green Rovers FC .... Page 14
Gateshead FC .... Page 15
Grays Athletic FC .... Page 16
Hayes & Yeading United FC .... Page 17
Histon FC .... Page 18
Kettering Town FC .... Page 19
Kidderminster Harriers FC .... Page 20
Luton Town FC .... Page 21
Mansfield Town FC .... Page 22
Oxford United FC .... Page 23
Rushden & Diamonds FC .... Page 24
Salisbury City FC .... Page 25
Stevenage Borough FC .... Page 26
Tamworth FC .... Page 27
Wrexham FC .... Page 28
York City FC .... Page 29

AFC WIMBLEDON

Founded: 2002
Former Names: Originally formed as Wimbledon Old Centrals (1889-1905) who later became Wimbledon FC
Nickname: 'The Dons'
Ground: The Cherry Red Records Fans' Stadium – Kingsmeadow, Jack Goodchild Way, 422A Kingston Road, Kingston-upon-Thames, Surrey KT1 3PB
Record Attendance: 4,722 (2009)

Pitch Size: 115 × 80 yards
Ground Capacity: 4,700
Seating Capacity: 1,277
Colours: Shirts and Shorts are Blue with Yellow trim
Telephone Nº: (020) 8547-3528
Fax Number: 0808 280-0816
Web site: www.afcwimbledon.co.uk

GENERAL INFORMATION

Car Parking: At the ground
Coach Parking: At the ground
Nearest Railway Station: Norbiton (1 mile)
Nearest Bus Station: Kingston
Club Shop: At the ground
Opening Times: Matchdays only
Telephone Nº: (020) 8547-3528
Police Telephone Nº: (020) 8541-1212

GROUND INFORMATION

Away Supporters' Entrances & Sections:
No usual segregation

ADMISSION INFO (2009/2010 PRICES)

Adult Standing: £12.00
Adult Seating: £14.00 – £16.00
Concessionary Standing: £6.00
Concessionary Seating: £7.00 – £8.00
Under-16s Standing: £2.00
Under-16s Seating: £3.00 – £4.00
Programme Price: £2.50

DISABLED INFORMATION

Wheelchairs: Accommodated around the ground
Helpers: Please phone the club for information
Prices: Please phone the club for information
Disabled Toilets: Yes
Contact: (020) 8547-3528 (Bookings are necessary)

Travelling Supporters' Information:
Routes: Exit the M25 at Junction 10 and take the A3 to the New Malden/Worcester Park turn-off and turn into Malden Road (A2043). Follow Malden Road to the mini-roundabout and turn left into Kingston Road. Kingsmeadow is situated approximately 1 mile up the Kingston Road, on the left-hand side and is signposted from the mini-roundabout.

ALTRINCHAM FC

Founded: 1891
Former Names: Broadheath FC
Nickname: 'The Robins'
Ground: Moss Lane, Altrincham   WA15 8AP
Record Attendance: 10,275 (February 1925)
Pitch Size: 110 × 74 yards

Colours: Red and White striped shirts, Black shorts
Telephone Nº: (0161) 928-1045
Daytime Phone Nº: (0161) 928-1045
Fax Number: (0161) 926-9934
Ground Capacity: 6,085
Seating Capacity: 1,154
Web site: www.altrinchamfc.com

GENERAL INFORMATION

Supporters Trust: Brian Flynn, c/o Club
Telephone Nº: –
Car Parking: Limited street parking
Coach Parking: By Police Direction
Nearest Railway Station: Altrincham (15 minutes walk)
Nearest Bus Station: Altrincham
Club Shop: Inside the ground
Opening Times: Matchdays only. Opens one hour prior to the start of the game.
Telephone Nº: (0161) 928-1045
Police Telephone Nº: (0161) 872-5050

GROUND INFORMATION

Away Supporters' Entrances & Sections:
Hale End turnstiles and accommodation

ADMISSION INFO (2009/2010 PRICES)

Adult Standing: £13.00
Adult Seating: £15.00
Concessionary Standing: £8.00
Concessionary Seating: £9.00
Ages 12-16 years Standing/Seating: £5.00
Under-12s Standing/Seating: £2.00
Programme Price: £2.00

DISABLED INFORMATION

Wheelchairs: 3 spaces are available each for home and away fans adjacent to the Away dugout
Helpers: Admitted
Prices: Free for the disabled. £12.00 for helpers
Disabled Toilets: Yes
Contact: (0161) 928-1045   (Bookings are necessary)

Travelling Supporters' Information:
Routes: Exit the M56 at either Junction 6 or 7 and following the signs Altrincham FC.

BARROW FC

Founded: 1901
Former Names: None
Nickname: 'Bluebirds'
Ground: Holker Street Stadium, Barrow-in-Furness, Cumbria   LA14 5UQ
Record Attendance: 16,874 (1954)
Pitch Size: 110 × 75 yards

Colours: White shirts with Blue shorts
Telephone Nº: (01229) 823061
Fax Number: (01229) 823061
Ground Capacity: 4,057
Seating Capacity: 928
Web site: www.barrowafc.com

GENERAL INFORMATION
Supporters Club: Bill Ablitt, c/o Club
Telephone Nº: (01229) 471617
Car Parking: Street Parking, Popular Side Car Park and Soccer Bar Car Park
Coach Parking: Adjacent to the ground
Nearest Railway Station: Barrow Central (½ mile)
Nearest Bus Station: ½ mile
Club Shop: At the ground
Opening Times: Monday to Friday 9.00am – 3.30pm and Saturdays 10.00am – 2.00pm
Telephone Nº: (01229) 823061
Police Telephone Nº: (01229) 824532

GROUND INFORMATION
Away Supporters' Entrances & Sections:
West Terrace (not covered)

ADMISSION INFO (2009/2010 PRICES)
Adult Standing: £13.00
Adult Seating: £14.00
Concessionary Standing: £10.00
Concessionary Seating: £11.00
Under-16s Standing/Seating: £5.00
Programme Price: £2.00

DISABLED INFORMATION
Wheelchairs: 6 spaces available in the Disabled Area
Helpers: Admitted
Prices: Normal prices apply
Disabled Toilets: Available
Contact: (01229) 823061   (Bookings are not necessary)

Travelling Supporters' Information:
Routes: Exit the M6 at Junction 36 and take the A590 through Ulverston. Using the bypass, follow signs for Barrow. After approximately 5 miles, turn left into Wilkie Road and the ground is on the right.

CAMBRIDGE UNITED FC

Founded: 1912
Former Name: Abbey United FC (1912-1951)
Nickname: 'U's' 'United'
Ground: The Trade Recruitment Stadium,
Newmarket Road, Cambridge   CB5 8LN
Ground Capacity: 8,339
Seating Capacity: 4,376

Pitch Size: 110 × 72 yards
Record Attendance: 14,000 (1st May 1970)
Colours: Amber shirts, Black shorts
Telephone Nº: (01223) 566500
Ticket Office: (01223) 566500
Fax Number: (01223) 729220
Web Site: www.cambridgeunited.com

GENERAL INFORMATION

Car Parking: Street parking only
Coach Parking: Coldhams Road
Nearest Railway Station: Cambridge (2 miles)
Nearest Bus Station: Cambridge City Centre
Club Shop: At the ground
Opening Times: Monday to Friday 9.00am to 5.00pm and
Matchdays 11.00am to kick-off
Telephone Nº: (01223) 566500
Police Telephone Nº: (01223) 358966

GROUND INFORMATION

Away Supporters' Entrances & Sections:
Coldham Common turnstiles 20-22 – Habbin Terrace (South)
and South Stand (Seating) turnstiles 23-26

ADMISSION INFO (2009/2010 PRICES)

Adult Standing: £15.00
Adult Seating: £16.00 – £18.00
Child Standing: £5.00
Child Seating: £6.00 (in the Family Stand) or £9.00–£10.00
Concessionary Standing: £11.00
Concessionary Seating: £12.00 – £13.00
Programme Price: £3.00

DISABLED INFORMATION

Wheelchairs: 19 spaces in total for Home fans in the
disabled sections, in front of Main Stand and in the North
Terrace. 16 spaces for Away fans in the South Stand.
Helpers: One helper admitted per disabled fan
Prices: £9.00 for the disabled. Free of charge for helpers
Disabled Toilets: At the rear of the disabled section
Contact: (01223) 566500   (Bookings are necessary)

Travelling Supporters' Information: Routes: From the North: Take the A1 and A14 to Cambridge and then head towards Newmarket. Turn off onto the B1047, signposted for Cambridge Airport, Horningsea and Fen Ditton. Turn right at the top of the slip road and travel through Fen Ditton. Turn right at the traffic lights at the end of the village. Go straight on at the roundabout onto Newmarket Road. The ground is 500 yards on the left; From the South and East: Take the A10 or A130 to the M11. Head North to the A14. Then as from the North; From the West: Take the A422 to Cambridge and join the A14. Then as from North.
Bus Services: Services from the Railway Station to the City Centre and Nº 3 from the City Centre to the Ground.

CHESTER CITY FC

Founded: 1885
Former Names: Chester FC
Nickname: 'Blues' 'City'
Ground: Deva Stadium, Bumpers Lane, Chester, CH1 4LT
Telephone Nº: (01244) 371376
Record Attendance: 5,987 (17th April 2004)
Pitch Size: 115 × 75 yards

Colours: Blue and White striped shirts, Blue shorts
Ticket Office: (01244) 371376
Fax Number: (01244) 390265
Ground Capacity: 5,556
Seating Capacity: 4,170
Web site: www.chestercityfc.net

GENERAL INFORMATION

Car Parking: Ample available at the ground (£3.00)
Coach Parking: Available at the ground
Nearest Railway Station: Chester (2 miles)
Nearest Bus Station: Chester (1½ miles)
Club Shop: At the ground
Opening Times: Weekdays & matchdays 10.00am–5.00pm
Telephone Nº: (01244) 371376
Police Telephone Nº: (01244) 350222

GROUND INFORMATION

Away Supporters' Entrances & Sections:
South Stand for covered seating and also part of the West Stand

ADMISSION INFO (2009/2010 PRICES)

Adult Standing: £15.00
Adult Seating: £15.00
Senior Citizen Seating/Standing: £10.00
Under-16s Seating/Standing: £5.00
Programme Price: £2.50

DISABLED INFORMATION

Wheelchairs: 32 spaces for wheelchairs (with 40 helpers) in the West Stand and East Stand
Helpers: One helper admitted per disabled person
Prices: Concessionary prices for the disabled. Free for helpers
Disabled Toilets: Available in West and East Stands
Contact: (01244) 371376 (Bookings are necessary)

Travelling Supporters' Information:
Routes: From the North: Take the M56, A41 or A56 into the Town Centre and then follow Queensferry (A548) signs into Sealand Road. Turn left at the traffic lights by 'Texas' into Bumpers Lane – the ground is ½ mile at the end of the road; From the East: Take the A54 or A51 into the Town Centre (then as North); From the South: Take the A41 or A483 into Town Centre (then as North); From the West: Take the A55, A494 or A548 and follow Queensferry signs towards Birkenhead (A494) and after 1¼ miles bear left onto the A548 (then as North); From the M6/M56 (Avoiding Town Centre): Take the M56 to Junction 16 (signposted Queensferry), turn left at the roundabout onto A5117, signposted Wales. At the next roundabout turn left onto the A5480 (signposted Chester) and after approximately 3 miles take the 3rd exit from the roundabout (signposted Sealand Road Industrial Parks). Go straight across 2 sets of traffic lights into Bumpers Lane. The ground is ½ mile on the right.

CRAWLEY TOWN FC

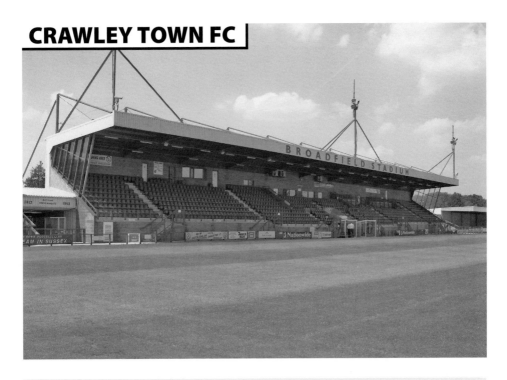

Founded: 1896
Former Names: None
Nickname: 'Red Devils'
Ground: Broadfield Stadium, Brighton Road, Crawley, Sussex   RH11 9RX
Record Attendance: 4,516 (2004)
Pitch Size: 110 × 72 yards

Colours: Red shirts and shorts
Telephone Nº: (01293) 410000 (Ground)
Daytime Nº: (01293) 410000 (10.00am – 4.00pm)
Fax Number: (01293) 410002
Ground Capacity: 4,941
Seating Capacity: 1,150
Web site: www.crawleytownfc.net

GENERAL INFORMATION

Supporters Club: Alain Harper, 33 Nuthurst Close, Ifield, Crawley, Sussex
Telephone Nº: (01293) 511764
Car Parking: 350 spaces available at the ground
Coach Parking: At the ground
Nearest Railway Station: Crawley (1 mile)
Nearest Bus Station: By the Railway Station
Club Shop: At the ground
Opening Times: Weekdays 10.00am to 4.00pm; Saturday matches 12.00pm to kick-off then one hour after the game; Mid-week matches 6.00pm to kick-off then one hour after the game
Telephone Nº: (01293) 410000
Police Telephone Nº: (08456) 070999

GROUND INFORMATION

Away Supporters' Entrances & Sections:
No usual segregation

ADMISSION INFO (2009/2010 PRICES)

Adult Standing: £13.00
Adult Seating: £16.00 (£35.00 in the Executive Area)
Child Standing: £1.00
Child Seating: £6.00 (£17.00 in the Executive Area)
Senior Citizen/Student Standing: £9.00
Senior Citizen/Student Seating: £12.00 (£26.00 in the Executive Area)
Programme Price: £2.50

DISABLED INFORMATION

Wheelchairs: Accommodated in the disabled section of the Main Stand (Lift access available)
Helpers: One helper admitted per disabled fan
Prices: Normal prices apply
Disabled Toilets: Available
Contact: (01293) 410000 (Bookings are not necessary)

Travelling Supporters' Information:
Routes: Exit the M23 at Junction 11 and take the A23 towards Crawley. After ¼ mile, the Stadium is on the left. Take the first exit at the roundabout for the Stadium entrance.

EASTBOURNE BOROUGH FC

Founded: 1963
Former Names: Langney Sports FC
Nickname: 'The Sports'
Ground: Priory Lane Stadium, Langney Sports Club, Priory Lane, Eastbourne BN23 7QH
Record Attendance: 3,770 (5th November 2005)
Pitch Size: 115 × 72 yards

Colours: Red shirts with Black shorts
Telephone Nº: (01323) 766265
Fax Number: (01323) 741627
Ground Capacity: 4,100
Seating Capacity: 542
Web site: www.ebfc.co.uk

GENERAL INFORMATION

Supporters Club: Yes – c/o Club
Telephone Nº: (01323) 766265
Car Parking: Around 400 spaces available at the ground
Coach Parking: At the ground
Nearest Railway Station: Pevensey & Westham (1½ miles but no public transport to the ground)
Nearest Bus Station: Eastbourne (Service 6A to ground)
Club Shop: At the ground
Opening Times: Wednesday to Friday and Matchdays 11.00am to 1.00pm
Telephone Nº: (01323) 766265
Police Telephone Nº: (0845) 607-0999

GROUND INFORMATION

Away Supporters' Entrances & Sections:
No usual segregation

ADMISSION INFO (2009/2010 PRICES)

Adult Standing: £13.00
Adult Seating: £13.00
Child Standing: £4.00 (Under-16s)
Child Seating: £4.00 (Under-16s)
Senior Citizen Standing: £9.00
Senior Citizen Seating: £9.00
Programme Price: £2.00

DISABLED INFORMATION

Wheelchairs: 6 spaces available
Helpers: Admitted
Prices: Normal prices apply
Disabled Toilets: Available
Contact: (01323) 766265 (Bookings are necessary)

Travelling Supporters' Information:
Routes: From the North: Exit the A22 onto the Polegate bypass, signposted A27 Eastbourne, Hastings & Bexhill. *Take the 2nd exit at the next roundabout for Stone Cross and Westham (A22) then the first exit at the following roundabout signposted Stone Cross and Westham. Turn right after ½ mile into Friday Street (B2104). At the end of Friday Street, turn left at the double mini-roundabout into Hide Hollow (B2191), passing Eastbourne Crematorium on your right. Turn right at the roundabout into Priory Road, and Priory Lane is about 200 yards down the road on the left; Approaching on the A27 from Brighton: Turn left at the Polegate traffic lights then take 2nd exit at the large roundabout to join the bypass. Then as from *.

EBBSFLEET UNITED FC

Founded: 1946
Former Names: Gravesend & Northfleet United FC, Gravesend United FC and Northfleet United FC
Nickname: 'The Fleet'
Ground: Stonebridge Road, Northfleet, Gravesend, Kent DA11 9GN
Record Attendance: 12,063 (1963)

Colours: Reds shirts with White shorts
Telephone Nº: (01474) 533796
Fax Number: (01474) 324754
Pitch Size: 112 × 72 yards
Ground Capacity: 5,258
Seating Capacity: 1,220
Web site: www.ebbsfleetunited.co.uk

GENERAL INFORMATION

Supporters Club: c/o Club
Telephone Nº: (01474) 533796
Car Parking: Ebbsfleet International Car Park C (when available) and also street parking
Coach Parking: At the ground
Nearest Railway Station: Northfleet (5 minutes walk)
Nearest Bus Station: Bus Stop outside the ground
Club Shop: At the ground
Opening Times: Matchdays only
Telephone Nº: (01474) 533796
Police Telephone Nº: (01474) 564346

GROUND INFORMATION

Away Supporters' Entrances & Sections:
Only some games are segregated – contact club for details

ADMISSION INFO (2009/2010 PRICES)

Adult Standing: £15.00
Adult Seating: £17.00
Senior Citizen/Child Standing: £8.00
Senior Citizen/Child Seating: £10.00
Note: An Under-16s season ticket is available for £23.00
Programme Price: £2.50

DISABLED INFORMATION

Wheelchairs: 6 spaces are available in the Disabled Area in front of the Main Stand
Helpers: Admitted free of charge
Prices: Please phone the club for information
Disabled Toilets: Available in the Main Stand
Contact: (01474) 533796 (Bookings are necessary)

Travelling Supporters' Information:
Routes: Take the A2 to the Northfleet/Southfleet exit and follow signs for Northfleet (B262). Go straight on at the first roundabout then take the 2nd exit at the 2nd roundabout into Thames Way and follow the football signs for the ground.

FOREST GREEN ROVERS FC

Founded: 1890
Former Names: Stroud FC
Nickname: 'The Rovers'
Ground: The New Lawn, Nympsfield Road,
Forest Green, Nailsworth, Gloucestershire, GL6 0ET
Record Attendance: 4,836 (3rd January 2009)
Pitch Size: 110 × 70 yards

Colours: Black and White striped shirts, Black shorts
Telephone Nº: (01453) 834860
Fax Number: (01453) 835291
Ground Capacity: 5,147
Seating Capacity: 2,500
Web site: www.fgrfc.co.uk

GENERAL INFORMATION

Supporters Club: Brian John Fream, c/o Club
Telephone Nº: (01453) 834860
Car Parking: At the ground
Coach Parking: At the ground
Nearest Railway Station: Stroud (4 miles)
Nearest Bus Station: Nailsworth
Club Shop: At the ground
Opening Times: Matchdays only
Telephone Nº: (01453) 834860
Police Telephone Nº: 0845 090-1234

GROUND INFORMATION

Away Supporters' Entrances & Sections:
South Stand

ADMISSION INFO (2009/2010 PRICES)

Adult Standing: £13.00
Adult Seating: £15.00
Senior Citizen Standing: £8.00
Senior Citizen Seating: £10.00
Child Standing: £5.00
Child Seating: £7.00
Programme Price: £2.50

DISABLED INFORMATION

Wheelchairs: Accommodated in the Main Stand
Helpers: Admitted
Prices: Normal prices for the disabled. Free for helpers
Disabled Toilets: Yes
Contact: (01453) 834860 (Enquiries necessary at least 72 hours in advance)

Travelling Supporters' Information:
Routes: The ground is located 4 miles south of Stroud on the A46 to Bath. Upon entering Nailsworth, turn into Spring Hill at the mini-roundabout and the ground is approximately ½ mile up the hill on the left.

GATESHEAD FC

Founded: 1930 (Reformed in 1977)	**Colours**: White shirts with Black shorts
Former Names: Gateshead United FC	**Telephone Nº**: (0191) 478-3883
Nickname: 'Tynesiders'	**Daytime Phone Nº**: (0191) 373-7014
Ground: International Stadium, Neilson Road,	**Fax Number**: (0191) 477-1315
Gateshead NE10 0EF	**Ground Capacity**: 11,750
Record Attendance: 11,750 (1995)	**Seating Capacity**: 11,750
Pitch Size: 110 × 70 yards	**Web site**: www.gateshead-fc.com

GENERAL INFORMATION

Supporters Club: c/o Club
Telephone Nº: –
Car Parking: At the stadium
Coach Parking: At the stadium
Nearest Railway Station: Gateshead Stadium Metro (½ mile); Newcastle (British Rail) 1½ miles
Nearest Bus Station: Heworth Interchange (½ mile)
Club Shop: At the stadium
Opening Times: Matchdays only
Telephone Nº: (0191) 478-3883
Police Telephone Nº: (0191) 232-3451

GROUND INFORMATION

Away Supporters' Entrances & Sections:
Tyne & Wear County Stand North End

ADMISSION INFO (2009/2010 PRICES)

Adult Seating: £12.00
Senior Citizen/Concessionary Seating: £7.00
Under-16s Seating: £2.00 if accompanying a paying adult
Programme Price: £2.50

DISABLED INFORMATION

Wheelchairs: 5 spaces available each for home and away fans by the trackside – Level access with automatic doors
Helpers: Please phone the club for information
Prices: Please phone the club for information
Disabled Toilets: Available in the Reception Area and on the 1st floor concourse – accessible by lift.
Contact: (0191) 478-3883   (Bookings are necessary)

Travelling Supporters' Information:
Routes: From the South: Take the A1(M) to Washington Services and fork right onto the A194(M) signposted Tyne Tunnel. At the next roundabout, turn left onto the A184 signposted for Gateshead. The Stadium is on the right after 3 miles.

GRAYS ATHLETIC FC

Founded: 1890
Former Names: None
Nickname: 'The Blues'
Ground: The New Recreation Ground, Bridge Road, Grays, Essex   RM17 6BZ
Record Attendance: 9,500 (1959)
Pitch Size: 110 × 71 yards

Colours: Blue shirts and shorts
Telephone Nº: (01375) 377753
Fax Number: (01375) 391649
Ground Capacity: 4,134
Seating Capacity: 1,200
Web site: www.graysathletic.co.uk

GENERAL INFORMATION

Supporters Association: c/o Club
Telephone Nº: (01375) 377753
Car Parking: Town Centre Car Parks close to the ground
Coach Parking: Car Parks close to the ground
Nearest Railway Station: Grays
Nearest Bus Station: Grays
Club Shop: At the ground
Opening Times: Matchdays only
Telephone Nº: (01375) 377753
Police Telephone Nº: (01375) 391212

GROUND INFORMATION

Away Supporters' Entrances & Sections:
Bradbourne Road entrances and accommodation just off Clarence Road

ADMISSION INFO (2009/2010 PRICES)

Adult Standing: £20.00
Adult Seating: £20.00
Concessionary Standing: £10.00
Concessionary Seating: £10.00
Student Standing/Seating: £10.00
Programme Price: £2.00

DISABLED INFORMATION

Wheelchairs: Accommodated in the Main Stand
Helpers: One admitted free of charge per disabled fan
Prices: Please phone the club for information
Disabled Toilets: Three available
Contact: (01375) 377753   (Bookings are recommended)

Travelling Supporters' Information:
Routes: Exit the M25 at Junction 30 and take the A13 towards Southend. At the Grays exit, follow signs to the town centre. Upon reaching the one-way system, keep to the left and continue uphill for about ½ miles before turning right into Bridge Road. The ground is then on the right.

HAYES & YEADING UNITED FC

Founded: 2007
Former Names: Formed by the amalgamation of Hayes FC and Yeading FC in 2007
Nickname: 'United'
Ground: Church Road, Hayes, Middlesex UB3 2LE
Record Attendance: 15,370 (10th February 1951)
Pitch Size: 117 × 70 yards

Colours: Red shirts with Black shorts
Telephone Nº: (020) 8573-2075
Fax Number: (020) 8573-0933
Ground Capacity: 4,300
Seating Capacity: 500
Web site: www.hyufc.net

GENERAL INFORMATION

Supporters Club: Lee Hermitage, c/o Hayes & Yeading United FC
Telephone Nº: (020) 8573-2075
Car Parking: 300 spaces available at the ground
Coach Parking: By arrangement
Nearest Railway Station: Hayes & Harlington (1 mile)
Nearest Bus Station: Hayes
Club Shop: At the ground
Opening Times: Matchdays only. Saturday matches from 2.00pm–5.00pm. Weekday matches from 6.45pm–9.30pm
Telephone Nº: (020) 8573-2075
Police Telephone Nº: (020) 8900-7212

GROUND INFORMATION

Away Supporters' Entrances & Sections:
Church Road End when segregated (not usual)

ADMISSION INFO (2009/2010 PRICES)

Adult Standing: £12.00
Adult Seating: £14.00
Child/Senior Citizen Standing: £7.00
Child/Senior Citizen Seating: £9.00
Programme Price: £2.00

DISABLED INFORMATION

Wheelchairs: Accommodated as necessary
Helpers: Admitted
Prices: £14.00 for the disabled but a helper is admitted free of charge with each paying disabled fan
Disabled Toilets: Available
Contact: (020) 8573-2075   (Bookings are not necessary)

Travelling Supporters' Information:
Routes: From the A40: Approaching London, take the Ruislip junction – turn right onto the B455 Ruislip Road to the White Hart Roundabout. Take the Hayes bypass to Uxbridge Road (A4020), turn right, then Church Road is ¾ mile on the left, opposite the Adam & Eve pub; From the M4: Exit at Junction 3 and take the A312 to Parkway towards Southall, then the Hayes bypass to Uxbridge Road (A4020). Turn left, then as above.

HISTON FC

Founded: 1904
Former Names: Histon Institute FC
Nickname: 'The Stutes'
Ground: The Glass World Stadium, Bridge Road, Impington, Cambridge CB4 9PH
Record Attendance: 6,400 (1956)
Pitch Size: 110 × 75 yards

Colours: Red and Black striped shirts, Black shorts
Telephone Nº: (01223) 237373
Fax Number: (01223) 237373
Ground Capacity: 4,100
Seating Capacity: 1,626
Web site: www.histonfc.co.uk

GENERAL INFORMATION

Supporters Club: Yes
Telephone Nº: (01223) 846455 (Jenny Wells)
Car Parking: Permit holders and disabled parking only at the ground. Check web site for details of fans parking
Coach Parking: For team coaches only
Nearest Railway Station: Cambridge (4 miles)
Nearest Bus Station: Cambridge (4 miles) (Use Citi Seven service for the ground)
Club Shop: At the ground
Opening Times: Three hours prior to kick-off for both Saturday and evening matches.
Telephone Nº: (01223) 237373

GROUND INFORMATION

Away Supporters' Entrances & Sections:
No usual segregation

ADMISSION INFO (2009/2010 PRICES)

Adult Standing: £13.00
Adult Seating: £14.00
Child Standing: £3.00
Child Seating: £4.00
Senior Citizen Standing: £7.00
Senior Citizen Seating: £8.00
Programme Price: £2.50

DISABLED INFORMATION

Wheelchairs: 6 spaces available in the home section and 6 spaces available in the away section
Helpers: Admitted
Prices: Concessionary prices for disabled. Free for helpers
Disabled Toilets: Available in both the home and away sections
Contact: Mac McDonald (Club safety officer) 07730 557021

Travelling Supporters' Information:
Routes: Exit the M11 at Junction 14 and follow the A14 eastwards. Take the first exit onto the B1049 (signposted Histon & Cottenham). Turn left at the traffic lights at the top of the slip road and pass the Holiday Inn on the right. Continue over the bridge and the entrance to the ground is on the right.

KETTERING TOWN FC

Founded: 1872
Former Names: Kettering FC
Nickname: 'The Poppies'
Ground: Elgood's Brewery Arena, Rockingham Road, Kettering, Northants NN16 9AW
Record Attendance: 11,526 (1947-48)
Pitch Size: 110 × 70 yards

Colours: Red shirts and shorts
Telephone Nº: (01536) 483028/517013
Daytime Phone Nº: (01536) 517013
Fax Number: (01536) 412273
Ground Capacity: Approximately 5,300
Seating Capacity: Approximately 1,550
Web site: www.ketteringtownfc.co.uk
E-mail: info@ketteringtownfc.co.uk

GENERAL INFORMATION

Supporters Club: c/o Club
Car Parking: At the ground
Coach Parking: As directed by the club
Nearest Railway Station: Kettering (1½ miles)
Nearest Bus Station: Kettering (1 mile)
Club Shop: At the ground. Also in Newlands Centre, Kettering
Opening Times: Shop hours in the Town Centre shop and at the ground on Matchdays
Telephone Nº: (01536) 510421
Police Telephone Nº: (01536) 411411

GROUND INFORMATION

Away Supporters' Entrances & Sections:
Main Stand, Entrance A when applicable

ADMISSION INFO (2009/2010 PRICES)

Adult Standing: £9.00 – £16.00
Adult Seating: £10.00 – £18.00
Senior Citizen Standing: £6.00 – £12.00
Senior Citizen Seating: £8.00 – £14.00
Under-16s Standing: £3.00 – £6.00
Under-16s Seating: £4.00 – £7.00
Note: Prices vary depending on the category of the game
Programme Price: £3.00

DISABLED INFORMATION

Wheelchairs: 7 spaces are available on the terracing adjacent to the Main Stand
Helpers: One helper admitted per wheelchair
Prices: Terrace prices for the disabled. Free for helpers
Disabled Toilets: Available
Contact: (01536) 483028 (Bookings are not necessary)

Travelling Supporters' Information:
Routes: To reach Kettering from the A1, M1 or M6, use the A14 to Junction 7, follow the A43 for 1 mile, turn right at the roundabout and the ground is 400 yards on the left on the A6003. (The ground is situated to the North of Kettering (1 mile) on the main A6003 Rockingham Road to Oakham).

KIDDERMINSTER HARRIERS FC

Founded: 1886
Nickname: 'Harriers'
Ground: Aggborough, Hoo Road, Kidderminster, Worcestershire DY10 1NB
Ground Capacity: 6,444
Seating Capacity: 3,143
Record Attendance: 9,155 (1948)

Pitch Size: 110 × 72 yards
Colours: Red and White halved shirts, White shorts
Telephone Nº: (01562) 823931
Fax Number: (01562) 827329
Web Site: www.harriers.co.uk

GENERAL INFORMATION

Car Parking: At the ground
Coach Parking: As directed
Nearest Railway Station: Kidderminster
Nearest Bus Station: Kidderminster Town Centre
Club Shop: At the ground
Opening Times: Weekdays and First Team Matchdays 9.00am to 5.00pm
Telephone Nº: (01562) 823931
Police Telephone Nº: –

GROUND INFORMATION

Away Supporters' Entrances & Sections:
John Smiths Stand Entrance D and South Terrace Entrance E

ADMISSION INFO (2009/2010 PRICES)

Adult Standing: £13.00
Adult Seating: £16.00
Senior Citizen Standing: £8.00   **Under-16s**: £5.00
Senior Citizen Seating: £11.00   **Under-16s**: £8.00
Note: Under-8s are admitted free with a paying adult
Programme Price: £2.50

DISABLED INFORMATION

Wheelchairs: Home fans accommodated at the front of the Main Stand, Away fans in front of the John Smiths Stand
Helpers: Admitted
Prices: £10.00 for each disabled fan plus one helper
Disabled Toilets: Available by the disabled area
Contact: (01562) 823931   (Bookings are not necessary)

Travelling Supporters' Information:
Routes: Exit the M5 at Junction 3 and follow the A456 to Kidderminster. The ground is situated close by the Severn Valley Railway Station so follow the brown Steam Train signs and turn into Hoo Road about 200 yards downhill of the station. Follow the road along for ¼ mile and the ground is on the left.

LUTON TOWN FC

Founded: 1885
Former Names: The club was formed by the amalgamation of Wanderers FC and Excelsior FC
Nickname: 'Hatters'
Ground: Kenilworth Road Stadium, 1 Maple Road, Luton LU4 8AW
Ground Capacity: 10,226 (All seats)
Record Attendance: 30,069 (4th March 1959)

Pitch Size: 110 × 72 yards
Colours: Shirts are White with Black trim, Black shorts
Telephone Nº: (01582) 411622
Ticket Office: (01582) 416976
Fax Number: (01582) 405070
Web Site: www.lutontown.co.uk

GENERAL INFORMATION

Car Parking: Street parking
Coach Parking: Luton Bus Station
Nearest Railway Station: Luton (1 mile)
Nearest Bus Station: Bute Street, Luton
Club Shop: Kenilworth Road Forecourt
Opening Times: 10.00am to 4.00pm
Telephone Nº: (01582) 411622
Police Telephone Nº: (01582) 401212

GROUND INFORMATION

Away Supporters' Entrances & Sections:
Oak Road for the Oak Stand

ADMISSION INFO (2009/2010 PRICES)

Adult Seating: £15.00 – £18.00
Under-10s Seating: £5.00
Under-17s Seating: £8.00
Under-22s Seating: £13.00
Senior Citizen Seating: £10.00 – £13.00
Note: Tickets are cheaper if bought prior to the matchday
Programme Price: £3.00

DISABLED INFORMATION

Wheelchairs: 32 spaces in total for Home and Away fans in the disabled section, Kenilworth Road End and Main Stand
Helpers: One helper admitted per disabled person
Prices: £15.00 for the disabled. Free of charge for helpers
Disabled Toilets: Available adjacent to disabled area
Commentaries are available for the blind
Contact: (01582) 416976 (Bookings are necessary)

Travelling Supporters' Information:
Routes: From the North and West: Exit the M1 at Junction 11 and follow signs for Luton (A505) into Dunstable Road. Follow the one-way system and turn right back towards Dunstable, take the second left into Ash Road for the ground; From the South and East: Exit the M1 at Junction 10 (or A6/A612) into Luton Town Centre and follow signs into Dunstable Road. After the railway bridge, take the sixth turning on the left into Ash Road for the ground.

MANSFIELD TOWN FC

Founded: 1897
Former Name: Mansfield Wesleyans FC (1897-1905)
Nickname: 'Stags'
Ground: Field Mill Ground, Quarry Lane, Mansfield, Nottinghamshire NG18 5DA
Ground Capacity: 10,000 (All seats)
Record Attendance: 24,467 (10th January 1953)
Pitch Size: 114 × 70 yards

Colours: Amber shirts with Royal Blue piping, Royal Blue shorts with Amber flash
Telephone Nº: (0870) 756-3160
Ticket Office: (0870) 756-3160
Fax Number: (01623) 482495
Web Site: www.mansfieldtown.net
E-mail: info@mansfieldtown.net

GENERAL INFORMATION

Car Parking: Large car park at the ground (£2.50)
Coach Parking: Adjacent to the ground
Nearest Railway Station: Mansfield (5 minutes walk)
Nearest Bus Station: Mansfield
Club Shop: In the South Stand of the Stadium
Opening Times: Weekdays 9.00am – 5.00pm and Matchdays 10.00am – 3.00pm
Telephone Nº: (0870) 756-3160
Police Telephone Nº: (01623) 420999

GROUND INFORMATION

Away Supporters' Entrances & Sections:
North Stand turnstiles for North Stand seating

ADMISSION INFO (2009/2010 PRICES)

Adult Seating: £16.00
Senior Citizen Seating: £10.00 – £11.00
Junior Seating: £8.00
Family Ticket: £20.00 (in the South Stand only)
Note: Under-4s are not admitted to the stadium
Programme Price: £2.50

DISABLED INFORMATION

Wheelchairs: 90 spaces available in total in the disabled sections in the North Stand, Quarry Street Stand & West Stand
Helpers: Admitted
Prices: £8.00 for the disabled. Helpers £15.00
Disabled Toilets: Available in the North Stand, West Stand and Quarry Lane Stand
Contact: (0870) 756-3160 (Please buy tickets in advance)

Travelling Supporters' Information:
Routes: From the North: Exit the M1 at Junction 29 and take the A617 to Mansfield. After 6¼ miles turn right at the Leisure Centre into Rosemary Street. Carry on to Quarry Lane and turn right; From the South and West: Exit the M1 at Junction 28 and take the A38 to Mansfield. After 6½ miles turn right at the crossroads into Belvedere Street then turn right after ¼ mile into Quarry Lane; From the East: Take the A617 to Rainworth, turn left at the crossroads after 3 miles into Windsor Road and turn right at the end into Nottingham Road, then left into Quarry Lane.

OXFORD UNITED FC

Founded: 1893
Former Names: Headington United FC (1893-1960)
Nickname: 'U's'
Ground: Kassam Stadium, Grenoble Road, Oxford, OX4 4XP
Ground Capacity: 12,500 (All seats)
Record Attendance: 22,730 (At the Manor Ground)

Pitch Size: 115 × 71 yards
Colours: Yellow shirts with Navy Blue shorts
Telephone Nº: (01865) 337500
Ticket Office: (01865) 337533
Fax Number: (01865) 337501
Web Site: www.oufc.co.uk

GENERAL INFORMATION

Car Parking: 2,000 free spaces available at the ground
Coach Parking: At the ground
Nearest Railway Station: Oxford (4 miles)
Nearest Bus Station: Oxford
Club Shop: At the ground
Opening Times: Monday to Friday 10.00am – 5.00pm and Matchdays from 10.00am until kick-off
Telephone Nº: (01865) 335310
Police Telephone Nº: (01865) 749909

GROUND INFORMATION

Away Supporters' Entrances & Sections:
North Stand turnstiles for North Stand accommodation.
Ticket office for away supporters is adjacent

ADMISSION INFO (2009/2010 PRICES)

Adult Seating: £16.00 – £19.50
Under-11s Seating: £5.50 – £11.00 (Under-7s free)
Senior Citizen/Under-16s Seating: £8.50 – £13.00
Note: Tickets are cheaper if bought before the matchday and other concessionary prices are available
Programme Price: £3.00

DISABLED INFORMATION

Wheelchairs: Accommodated in areas in the North, East and South Stands
Helpers: One helper admitted per disabled person
Prices: Normal prices for the disabled. One assistant admitted free of charge per disabled fan if required
Disabled Toilets: Available throughout the ground
Commentaries are available for the visually impaired
Contact: (01865) 337533 (Bookings are not necessary)

Travelling Supporters' Information:
Routes: From the Oxford Ring Road take the A423 towards Henley and Reading then turn left after ½ mile following signs for the Oxford Science Park. Bear left and go straight on at two roundabouts then the Stadium is on the left in Grenoble Road. The Kassam Stadium is clearly signposted on all major roads in Oxford.

RUSHDEN & DIAMONDS FC

Founded: 1992	**Record Attendance**: 6,431 (vs Leeds United in 1999)
Former Names: Formed by the amalgamation of Rushden Town FC and Irthlingborough Diamonds FC	**Pitch Size**: 111 × 74 yards
Nickname: 'Diamonds'	**Colours**: Shirts, shorts and socks are White with Blue and Red trim
Ground: Nene Park, Diamond Way, Irthlingborough, Northants NN9 5QF	**Telephone Nº**: (01933) 652000
	Ticket Office Nº: (01933) 652936
Ground Capacity: 6,441	**Fax Number**: (01933) 654190
Seating Capacity: 4,641	**Web Site**: www.thediamondsfc.com

GENERAL INFORMATION

Car Parking: At the ground (£3.00 charge)
Coach Parking: At the ground (£10.00 charge)
Nearest Railway Station: Wellingborough (5 miles)
Nearest Bus Station: Wellingborough
Club Shop: Yes – at the front of the Stadium
Opening Times: Weekdays 10.00am to 5.00pm; Matchdays 10.00am until kick-off then 30 minutes after the game.
Telephone Nº: (01933) 652000
Police Telephone Nº: (01933) 440333

GROUND INFORMATION

Away Supporters' Entrances & Sections:
Large following: Airwair Stand – enter via gates T/S/R
Smaller following: South Stand Block C5 – gates K/L

ADMISSION INFO (2009/2010 PRICES)

Adult Standing: £13.00 (Home fans only)
Adult Seating: £16.00
Concessionary Standing: £8.00
Concessionary Seating: £11.00
Under-16s Standing/Seating: £5.00
Note: Under-8s are admitted free with a paying adult
Programme Price: £3.00

DISABLED INFORMATION

Wheelchairs: Accommodated around the ground
Helpers: Admitted
Prices: £8.00 – £11.00 for the disabled with registered carers admitted free of charge
Disabled Toilets: Available around the ground
Contact: (01933) 652936 Matt Banyard (Bookings are preferred)

Travelling Supporters' Information:
Routes: The ground is located on the A6 about 350 yards north of the junction with the A45 (over the bridge). This is approximately 6 miles south of the A14.

SALISBURY CITY FC

Founded: 1947
Former Names: Salisbury FC
Nickname: 'The Whites'
Ground: The Raymond McEnhill Stadium, Partridge Way, Old Sarum, Salisbury, Wiltshire   SP4 6PU
Record Attendance: 3,100 (3rd December 2006)
Pitch Size: 115 × 76 yards

Colours: White shirts with Black shorts
Telephone Nº: (01722) 776655
Fax Number: (01722) 776666
Ground Capacity: 5,000
Seating Capacity: 500
Web site: www.salisburycity-fc.co.uk

GENERAL INFORMATION

Car Parking: At the ground
Coach Parking: At the ground
Nearest Railway Station: Salisbury (2½ miles)
Nearest Bus Station: Salisbury
Club Shop: At the ground + an online shop
Opening Times: Office Hours and Matchdays
Telephone Nº: (01722) 776655
Postal Sales: Yes
Police Telephone Nº: (01722) 411444

GROUND INFORMATION

Away Supporters' Entrances & Sections:
Portway End entrances and accommodation

ADMISSION INFO (2009/2010 PRICES)

Adult Standing: £13.00
Adult Seating: £15.00
Senior Citizen Standing: £9.00
Senior Citizen Seating: £11.00
Under-16s Standing: £3.00   (Students: £7.00)
Under-16s Seating: £5.00   (Students: £9.00)
Programme Price: £2.50

DISABLED INFORMATION

Wheelchairs: Accommodated in a special area in the Main Stand. A stairlift is available.
Helpers: Admitted free of charge
Prices: Normal prices apply for the disabled
Disabled Toilets: Available
Contact: (01722) 776655   (Bookings are necessary)

Travelling Supporters' Information:
Routes: The Stadium well signposted and is situated off the main A345 Salisbury to Amesbury road on the northern edge of the City, 2 miles from the City Centre.

STEVENAGE BOROUGH FC

Founded: 1976
Former Names: None
Nickname: 'Boro'
Ground: Lamex Stadium, Broadhall Way, Stevenage, Hertfordshire   SG2 8RH
Record Attendance: 8,040 (25th January 1998)
Pitch Size: 110 × 70 yards

Colours: Red and White shirts with Red shorts
Telephone Nº: (01438) 223223
Daytime Phone Nº: (01438) 223223
Fax Number: (01438) 743666
Ground Capacity: 7,104
Seating Capacity: 3,404
Web site: www.stevenageborofc.com

GENERAL INFORMATION

Supporters Club: Mervyn Stoke Geddis, 21 Woodland Way, Stevenage
Telephone Nº: (01438) 313236
Car Parking: Fairlands Show Ground (opposite)
Coach Parking: At the ground
Nearest Railway Station: Stevenage (1 mile)
Nearest Bus Station: Stevenage
Club Shop: At the ground
Opening Times: Tuesday to Thursday and matchdays 10.00am to 5.00pm
Telephone Nº: 0870 811-2494
Police Telephone Nº: (01438) 757000

GROUND INFORMATION

Away Supporters' Entrances & Sections:
South Terrace entrances and accommodation

ADMISSION INFO (2009/2010 PRICES)

Adult Standing: £12.00
Adult Seating: £15.00
Child Standing: £5.00
Senior Citizen Standing: £10.00
Senior Citizen/Child Seating: £12.00
Programme Price: £2.50

DISABLED INFORMATION

Wheelchairs: 10 spaces available in total by the North Terrace
Helpers: Admitted
Prices: £9.00 for the disabled. Free of charge for helpers
Disabled Toilets: Yes
Contact: (01438) 223223   (Bookings are necessary)

Travelling Supporters' Information:
Routes: Exit the A1(M) at Junction 7 and take the B197. The ground is on the right at the 2nd roundabout.
Bus Routes: SB4 and SB5

TAMWORTH FC

Founded: 1933
Former Names: None
Nickname: 'The Lambs'
Ground: The Lamb Ground, Kettlebrook, Tamworth, B77 1AA
Record Attendance: 4,920 (3rd April 1948)
Pitch Size: 110 × 73 yards

Colours: Red shirts and shorts
Telephone Nº: (01827) 65798
Daytime Phone Nº: (01827) 65798
Fax Number: (01827) 62236
Ground Capacity: 4,118
Seating Capacity: 520
Web site: www.thelambs.co.uk

GENERAL INFORMATION

Supporters Club: Dave Brown, c/o Club
Car Parking: 200 spaces available at the ground – £1.00 per car or £10.00 per coach
Coach Parking: At the ground
Nearest Railway Station: Tamworth (½ mile)
Nearest Bus Station: Tamworth (½ mile)
Club Shop: At the ground
Opening Times: Weekdays & Matchdays 10.00am – 4.00pm
Telephone Nº: (01827) 65798
Police Telephone Nº: (01827) 61001

GROUND INFORMATION

Away Supporters' Entrances & Sections:
Gates 1 and 2 for Terracing, Gate 2A for seating

ADMISSION INFO (2009/2010 PRICES)

Adult Standing: £12.00
Adult Seating: £14.00
Child/Senior Citizen Standing: £7.00
Child/Senior Citizen Seating: £9.00
Programme Price: £2.00

DISABLED INFORMATION

Wheelchairs: Accommodated
Helpers: Admitted
Prices: Normal prices apply for Wheelchair disabled. Helpers are charged concessionary rates
Disabled Toilets: Yes
Contact: (01827) 65798 (Bookings are advisable)

Travelling Supporters' Information:
Routes: Exit the M42 at Junction 10 and take the A5/A51 to the town centre following signs for Town Centre/Snowdome. The follow signs for Kettlebrook and the ground is in Kettlebrook Road, 50 yards from the traffic island by the Railway Viaduct and the Snowdome. The ground is signposted from all major roads.

WREXHAM FC

Founded: 1872
Nickname: 'Red Dragons'
Ground: Racecourse Ground, Mold Road, Wrexham, North Wales   LL11 2AH
Ground Capacity: 10,500 (all seats) at present as the ground undergoes re-development
Record Attendance: 34,445 (26th January 1957)

Pitch Size: 111 × 71 yards
Colours: Red shirts with White shorts
Telephone Nº: (01978) 262129
Fax Number: (01978) 357821
Web Site: www.wrexhamafc.co.uk

GENERAL INFORMATION

Car Parking: Town car parks are nearby and also Glyndwr University (Mold End)
Coach Parking: By Police direction
Nearest Railway Station: Wrexham General (adjacent)
Nearest Bus Station: Wrexham (King Street)
Club Shop: At the ground, under the Main Stand
Opening Times: Monday to Saturday 9.00am to 5.00pm
Telephone Nº: (01978) 262129
Police Telephone Nº: (01978) 290222

GROUND INFORMATION

Away Supporters' Entrances & Sections:
Turnstiles 1-4 for the Yale Stand

ADMISSION INFO (2009/2010 PRICES)

Adult Seating: £17.00 – £18.00
Child Seating: £5.00
Senior Citizen Seating: £12.00
Note: Tickets are cheaper when purchased in advance
Programme Price: £3.00

DISABLED INFORMATION

Wheelchairs: 35 spaces in the Pryce Griffiths Stand
Helpers: One helper admitted per wheelchair
Prices: £10.00 for the disabled. Free of charge for helpers
Disabled Toilets: Available in the disabled section
Contact: (01978) 351332 (Tony Millington) (Please book)

Travelling Supporters' Information:
Routes: From the North and West: Take the A483 and the Wrexham bypass to the junction with the A541. Branch left at the roundabout and follow Wrexham signs into Mold Road; From the East: Take the A525 or A534 into Wrexham then follow the A541 signs into Mold Road; From the South: Take the the the M6, then the M54 and follow the A5 and A483 to the Wrexham bypass and the junction with the A541. Branch right at the roundabout and follow signs for the Town Centre.

YORK CITY FC

Founded: 1922
Nickname: 'Minstermen'
Ground: Kit Kat Crescent, York   YO30 7AQ
Ground Capacity: 9,496
Seating Capacity: 3,509
Record Attendance: 28,123   (5th March 1938)
Pitch Size: 115 × 74 yards

Colours: Red and Blue halved shirts, Blue shorts
Telephone Nº: (01904) 624447
Ticket Office: (01904) 624447   Extension 1
Fax Number: (01904) 631457
Web Site: www.ycfc.net

GENERAL INFORMATION

Car Parking: Street parking
Coach Parking: By Police direction
Nearest Railway Station: York (1 mile)
Nearest Bus Station: York
Club Shop: At the ground
Opening Times: Weekdays 10.30am – 2.30pm and
Saturday Matchdays 1.00pm–3.00pm and 4.40pm–5.30pm;
Evening matches open from 6.00pm
Telephone Nº: (01904) 624447 Extension 4
Police Telephone Nº: 0845 606-0247

GROUND INFORMATION

Away Supporters' Entrances & Sections:
Grosvenor Road turnstiles for Grosvenor Road End

ADMISSION INFO (2009/2010 PRICES)

Adult Standing: £14.00
Adult Seating: £15.00 – £17.00
Child Standing: £9.00
Child Seating: £6.00 – £11.00
Note: Concessions are available in the Family Stand
Programme Price: £3.00

DISABLED INFORMATION

Wheelchairs: 18 spaces in total for Home and Away fans in
the disabled section, in front of the Social Club
Helpers: One helper admitted per disabled person
Prices: £14.00 for the disabled. Free of charge for helpers
Disabled Toilets: Available at entrance to the disabled area
Contact: (01904) 624447 (Ext. 1) (Bookings not necessary)

Travelling Supporters' Information:
Routes: From the North: Take the A1 then the A59 following signs for York. Cross the railway bridge and turn left after 2 miles
into Water End. Turn right at the end following City Centre signs for nearly ½ mile then turn left into Bootham Crescent; From
the South: Take the A64 and turn left after Buckles Inn onto the Outer Ring Road. Turn right onto the A19, follow City Centre
signs for 1½ miles then turn left into Bootham Crescent; From the East: Take the Outer Ring Road turning left onto the A19.
Then as from the South; From the West: Take the Outer Ring Road turning right onto the A19. Then as from the South.

THE FOOTBALL CONFERENCE BLUE SQUARE NORTH

Address

Third Floor, Wellington House,
31-34 Waterloo Street, Birmingham   B2 5TJ

Phone (0121) 214-1950

Web site   www.footballconference.co.uk

Clubs for the 2009/2010 Season

AFC Telford .... Page 31
Alfreton Town FC .... Page 32
Blyth Spartans FC .... Page 33
Corby Town FC .... Page 34
Droylsden FC .... Page 35
Eastwood Town FC .... Page 36
Farsley Celtic FC .... Page 37
Fleetwood Town FC .... Page 38
Gainsborough Trinity FC .... Page 39
Gloucester City FC .... Page 40
Harrogate Town FC .... Page 41
Hinckley United FC .... Page 42
Hyde United FC .... Page 43
Ilkeston Town FC .... Page 44
Northwich Victoria FC .... Page 45
Redditch United FC .... Page 46
Solihull Moors FC .... Page 47
Southport FC .... Page 48
Stafford Rangers FC .... Page 49
Stalybridge Celtic FC .... Page 50
Vauxhall Motors FC .... Page 51
Workington FC .... Page 52

AFC TELFORD UNITED

Founded: 2004
Former Names: Formed after Telford United FC went out of business
Nickname: 'The Bucks'
Ground: The New Bucks Head Stadium, Watling Street, Wellington, Telford TF1 2TU
Record Attendance: 13,000 (1935)

Pitch Size: 110 × 74 yards
Colours: White shirts with Black shorts
Telehone Nº: (01952) 640064
Fax Number: (01952) 640021
Ground Capacity: 5,780
Seating Capacity: 2,280
Web site: www.telfordutd.co.uk

GENERAL INFORMATION

Supporters Club: None
Car Parking: At the ground
Coach Parking: At the ground
Nearest Railway Station: Wellington
Nearest Bus Station: Wellington
Club Shop: At the ground
Opening Times: Tuesdays 4.00pm to 6.00pm, Thursdays 4.30pm to 6.30pm and Saturday Matchdays from 1.30pm
Telephone Nº: –
Police Telephone Nº: 08457 444888

GROUND INFORMATION

Away Supporters' Entrances & Sections:
Frank Nagington Stand on the rare occasions when segregation is used

ADMISSION INFO (2009/2010 PRICES)

Adult Standing: £11.00
Adult Seating: £11.00
Child Standing: £1.00
Child Seating: £1.00
Senior Citizen/Concessionary Standing: £8.00
Senior Citizen/Concessionary Seating: £8.00
Programme Price: £2.00

DISABLED INFORMATION

Wheelchairs: Accommodated at the both ends of the ground
Helpers: Admitted
Prices: Normal prices apply
Disabled Toilets: Available
Contact: (01952) 640064 (Bookings are not necessary)

Travelling Supporters' Information:
Routes: Exit the M54 at Junction 6 and take the A518. Go straight on at the first roundabout, take the second exit at the next roundabout then turn left at the following roundabout. Follow the road round to the right then turn left into the car park.

ALFRETON TOWN FC

Founded: 1959
Former Names: None
Nickname: 'Reds'
Ground: The Impact Arena, North Street, Alfreton, Derbyshire
Record Attendance: 5,023 vs Matlock Town (1960)
Pitch Size: 110 × 75 yards

Colours: Red shirts and shorts
Telephone Nº: (01773) 830277
Fax Number: (01773) 836164
Ground Capacity: 5,000
Seating Capacity: 1,600
Web site: www.alfretontownfc.com

GENERAL INFORMATION
Supporters Club: Mark Thorpe, c/o Social Club
Telephone Nº: (01773) 836251
Car Parking: At the ground
Coach Parking: At the ground
Nearest Railway Station: Alfreton (½ mile)
Nearest Bus Station: Alfreton (5 minutes walk)
Club Shop: At the ground
Opening Times: Matchdays (including Youth & Reserves)
Telephone Nº: (01773) 830277
Police Telephone Nº: (01773) 570100

GROUND INFORMATION
Away Supporters' Entrances & Sections:
Segregation not usual but please check prior to the game

ADMISSION INFO (2009/2010 PRICES)
Adult Standing: £10.00
Adult Seating: £10.00
Senior Citizen/Junior Standing: £5.00
Senior Citizen/Junior Seating: £5.00
Programme Price: £2.00

DISABLED INFORMATION
Wheelchairs: Accommodated at the front of the Stand
Helpers: Admitted
Prices: Please phone the club for information
Disabled Toilets: Available
Contact: (01773) 830277 (Bookings are not necessary)

Travelling Supporters' Information:
Routes: Exit the M1 at Junction 28 and take the A38 signposted for Derby. After 2 miles take the sliproad onto the B600 then go right at the main road towards the town centre. After ½ mile turn left down North Street and the ground is on the right after 200 yards.

BLYTH SPARTANS FC

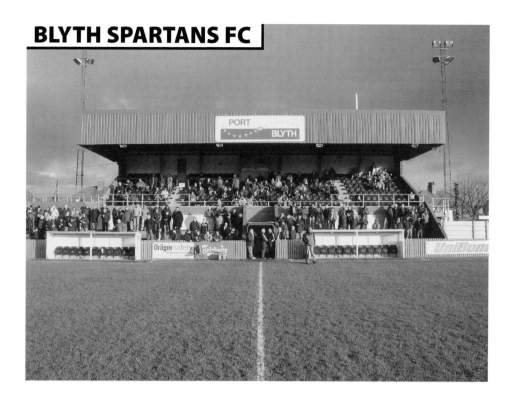

Founded: 1899
Former Names: None
Nickname: 'Spartans'
Ground: Croft Park, Blyth, Northumberland, NE24 3JE
Record Attendance: 10,186
Pitch Size: 110 × 70 yards

Colours: Green and White striped shirts, Black shorts
Telephone Nº: (01670) 352373 (Office)
Fax Number: (01670) 545592
Ground Capacity: 6,000
Seating Capacity: 540
Web site: www.blythspartansafc.co.uk

GENERAL INFORMATION

Supporters Club: Bobby Bell, c/o Club
Telephone Nº: (01670) 352373
Car Parking: At the ground
Coach Parking: At the ground
Nearest Railway Station: Newcastle
Nearest Bus Station: Blyth (5 minutes walk)
Club Shop: At the ground
Opening Times: Matchdays only
Telephone Nº: c/o (01670) 336379
Police Telephone Nº: (01661) 872555

GROUND INFORMATION

Away Supporters' Entrances & Sections:
No usual segregation

ADMISSION INFO (2009/2010 PRICES)

Adult Standing: £9.00
Adult Seating: £10.00
Child Standing: £5.00
Child Seating: £6.00
Programme Price: £1.50

DISABLED INFORMATION

Wheelchairs: Accommodated
Helpers: Please phone the club for information
Prices: Please phone the club for information
Disabled Toilets: Yes
Contact: (01670) 352373 (Bookings are necessary)

Travelling Supporters' Information:
Routes: Pass through the Tyne Tunnel and take the left lane for Morpeth (A19/A1). At the 2nd roundabout (after approximately 7 miles) take full right turn for the A189 (signposted Ashington). After 2 miles take the slip road (A1061 signposted Blyth). Follow signs for Blyth turning left at the caravan site. At the 2nd roundabout turn right and the ground is on the left.

CORBY TOWN FC

Founded: 1948
Former Names: None
Nickname: 'The Steelmen'
Ground: Rockingham Triangle Stadium, Rockingham Road, Corby NN17 2AE
Record Attendance: 2,240 vs Watford (1986/87)
Pitch Size: 110 × 70 yards

Colours: Black and White Striped shirts, Black shorts
Telephone Nº: (01536) 406640
Fax Number: (0116) 237-6162
Ground Capacity: 3,000
Seating Capacity: 964
Web site: www.corbytown.net

GENERAL INFORMATION

Supporters Club: None
Car Parking: Spaces for 250 cars at the ground
Coach Parking: At the ground
Nearest Railway Station: Kettering (8 miles)
Nearest Bus Station: Corby Town Centre
Club Shop: At the ground
Opening Times: Matchdays only – 1 hour before kick-off
Telephone Nº: (01536) 406640
Police Telephone Nº: (01252) 324545

GROUND INFORMATION

Away Supporters' Entrances & Sections:
No usual segregation

ADMISSION INFO (2009/2010 PRICES)

Adult Standing: £9.00
Adult Seating: £9.00
Child Standing: £2.00
Child Seating: £2.00
Senior Citizen Standing: £5.00
Senior Citizen Seating: £5.00
Programme Price: £2.00

DISABLED INFORMATION

Wheelchairs: Accommodated
Helpers: Admitted
Prices: Normal prices apply for the disabled and helpers
Disabled Toilets: Available
Contact: (01536) 406640   (Bookings are not necessary)

Travelling Supporters' Information:
Routes: From the North & East: Exit the A1(M) at junction 17 and take the A605 to Oundle then the A427 to Little Weldon. At the roundabout take the A6116 towards Rockingham and the ground is adjacent to Rockingham Castle near the junction with the A6003; From the South: Take the A14 to the junction with the A6116 and continue to the junction with the A6003 at Rockingham Castle; From the West: Take the A14 or A427 to the A6003 then continue north towards Rockingham to the junction with the A6116 where the ground is on the left.

DROYLSDEN FC

Founded: 1892
Former Names: None
Nickname: 'The Bloods'
Ground: Butchers Arms, Market Street, Droylsden, Manchester M43 7AY
Record Attendance: 5,400 (1973)
Pitch Size: 110 × 70 yards

Colours: Red shirts with Red shorts
Telephone Nº: (0161) 370-1426
Daytime Phone Nº: (0161) 370-1426
Fax Number: (0161) 370-8341
Ground Capacity: 3,500
Seating Capacity: 500
Web site: www.droylsdenfc.com

GENERAL INFORMATION

Supporters Club: c/o Club
Telephone Nº: –
Car Parking: Street parking only
Coach Parking: At the ground
Nearest Railway Station: Manchester Piccadilly
Nearest Bus Station: Ashton
Club Shop: At the ground
Opening Times: Matchdays only
Telephone Nº: (0161) 370-1426
Police Telephone Nº: (0161) 330-8321

GROUND INFORMATION

Away Supporters' Entrances & Sections:
No usual segregation

ADMISSION INFO (2009/2010 PRICES)

Adult Standing: £10.00
Adult Seating: £10.00
Concessionary Standing: £6.00
Concessionary Seating: £6.00
Note: Under-14s are admitted free of charge
Programme Price: £2.00

DISABLED INFORMATION

Wheelchairs: Accommodated beside the Stand
Helpers: Yes
Prices: Normal prices apply for the disabled and helpers
Disabled Toilets: Available
Contact: (0161) 370-1426 (Bookings are not necessary)

Travelling Supporters' Information:
Routes: Take the Manchester Outer Ring Road M60 and exit at Junction 23. Join the A635 towards Manchester and after the retail park on the left, take the centre lane, then turn right at the traffic lights onto the A662 signposted for Droylsden. At the next traffic lights, turn right onto Market Street and after 150 yards go straight on at the traffic lights. The entrance to the ground is 75 yards on the left.

EASTWOOD TOWN FC

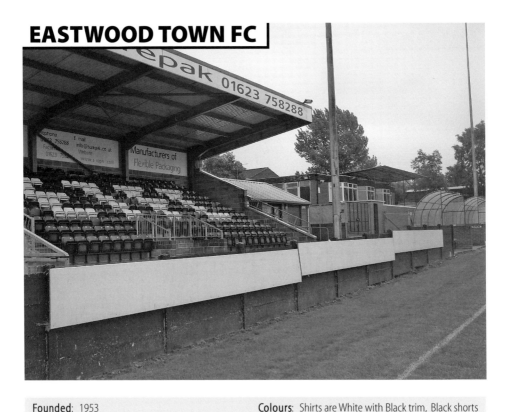

Founded: 1953
Former Names: None
Nickname: 'The Badgers'
Ground: Coronation Park, Chewton Street, Eastwood   NG16 3HB
Record Attendance: 2,723 (February 1965)
Pitch Size: 115 × 77 yards

Colours: Shirts are White with Black trim, Black shorts
Telephone Nº: (01773) 715823
Fax Number: (01773) 786186
Ground Capacity: 2,500
Seating Capacity: 550
Web site: www.eastwoodtownfc.co.uk

GENERAL INFORMATION
Supporters Club: c/o Club
Telephone Nº: (01773) 715823
Car Parking: At the ground
Coach Parking: At the ground
Nearest Railway Station: Langley Mill (1 mile)
Nearest Bus Station: Nottingham
Club Shop: At the ground
Opening Times: Matchdays only
Telephone Nº: (01773) 786186

GROUND INFORMATION
Away Supporters' Entrances & Sections:
No usual segregation

ADMISSION INFO (2009/2010 PRICES)
Adult Standing/Seating: £9.00
Under-16s Standing/Seating: £2.00
Senior Citizen Standing/Seating: £7.00
Note: Under-16s attending with a paying adult are admitted free of charge.
Programme Price: £2.00

DISABLED INFORMATION
Wheelchairs: Accommodated
Helpers: Admitted
Prices: Normal prices apply
Disabled Toilets: Available
Contact: (01773) 715823   (Bookings are not necessary)

Travelling Supporters' Information:
Routes: From the North: Exit the M1 at Junction 27 and take the 3rd exit at the roundabout towards Heanor (A608). Follow the road past the Sandhills Tavern to a T-junction signposted for Brinsley/Heanor and continue along the A608. Follow the road through Brinsley into Eastwood then turn left at the lights into Nottingham Road. Look for the Fire Station on the right, then take the first right into Chewton Street. The Ground is on the right after 150 metres; From the South: Exit the M1 at Junction 26 and follow the A610 towards Ripley. Exit the A610 at the first junction signposted for Ilkeston and turn right onto the B6010, following the signs for Eastwood. Take the first left after the Man In Space pub into Chewton Street. The ground is on the right.

FARSLEY CELTIC FC

Founded: 1908
Former Names: None
Nickname: 'Villagers'
Ground: Throstle Nest, Newlands, Farsley, Leeds, LS28 5BE
Record Attendance: 2,462 (2006)
Pitch Size: 110 × 67 yards

Colours: Blue shirts and shorts
Telephone Nº: (0113) 255-7292
Fax Number: (0113) 256-1517
Ground Capacity: 4,000
Seating Capacity: 500
Web site: www.farsleyceltic.net
e-mail: farsleyceltic1908@supanet.com

GENERAL INFORMATION
Car Parking: Available at the ground
Coach Parking: Available at the ground
Nearest Railway Station: New Pudsey (1 mile)
Nearest Bus Station: Pudsey (1 mile)
Club Shop: At the ground
Opening Times: Weekday evenings 6.00pm – 11.00pm and weekends noon until 11.00pm
Telephone Nº: (0113) 255-7292

GROUND INFORMATION
Away Supporters' Entrances & Sections:
No usual segregation

ADMISSION INFO (2009/2010 PRICES)
Adult Standing: £9.00
Adult Seating: £9.00
Senior Citizen/Student Standing: £4.00
Senior Citizen/Student Seating: £4.00
Child Standing: £1.00
Child Seating: £1.00
Programme Price: £2.00

DISABLED INFORMATION
Wheelchairs: Accommodated
Helpers: Please phone the club for information
Prices: Please phone the club for information
Disabled Toilets: Available
Contact: (0113) 255-7292   (Bookings are necessary)

Travelling Supporters' Information:
Routes: From the North: Take the A1 to Wetherby then the A58 to Leeds. After about 8 miles take the 3rd exit at the roundabout onto the A6120 Ring Road. Follow signs for Bradford for approximately 12 miles and at the 7th roundabout take the B6157 signposted Stanningley. Continue for ½ mile passing the Police Station on the left then turn left down New Street (at the Tradex Warehouse). Turn right into Newlands and the ground is situated at the end of the road next to a new housing development.

FLEETWOOD TOWN FC

Founded: 1977
Former Names: None (The club succeeded Fleetwood FC who existed from 1907-1977)
Nickname: 'The Fishermen'
Ground: Highbury Stadium, Park Avenue, Fleetwood FY7 8LP
Record Attendance: 6,150 vs Rochdale FC (1965)

Pitch Size: 112 × 71 yards
Colours: Red shirts with White sleeves, White shorts
Telephone Nº: (01253) 770702
Fax Number: (01253) 770702
Ground Capacity: 3,450
Seating Capacity: 550
Web site: www.fleetwoodtownfc.com

GENERAL INFORMATION

Car Parking: Spaces for 40 cars at the ground and also street parking
Coach Parking: At the ground
Nearest Railway Station: Poulton (7 miles)
Nearest Bus Station: Fleetwood
Club Shop: Sales via the club web site only
Opening Times: –
Telephone Nº: –

GROUND INFORMATION

Away Supporters' Entrances & Sections:
No usual segregation

ADMISSION INFO (2008/2009 PRICES)

Adult Standing: £10.00
Adult Seating: £10.00
Child Standing: £5.00
Child Seating: £5.00
Senior Citizen Standing: £5.00
Senior Citizen Seating: £5.00
Programme Price: £2.00

DISABLED INFORMATION

Wheelchairs: Accommodated
Helpers: Admitted
Prices: Normal prices apply for the disabled and helpers
Disabled Toilets: Available
Contact: (01253) 770702 (Bookings are necessary)

Travelling Supporters' Information:
Routes: Exit the M55 at Junction 3 and take the A585 to Fleetwood (approximately 11½ miles). Upon reaching Fleetwood, take the 1st exit at the Nautical College roundabout (with the statue of Eros in the middle) and continue for about 1 mile to the next roundabout. Take the 6th exit onto Hatfield Avenue and after about ½ mile (when the road bends to the right)m turn left into Nelson Road. The ground is situated on the left after 100 yards.

GAINSBOROUGH TRINITY FC

Founded: 1873
Former Names: None
Nickname: 'The Blues'
Ground: Northolme, Gainsborough, Lincolnshire, DN21 2QW
Record Attendance: 9,760 (1948)
Pitch Size: 111 × 71 yards

Colours: Blue shirts with White shorts
Telephone Nº: (01427) 613295 or 612791
Clubhouse Phone Nº: (01427) 613688
Fax Number: (01427) 613295
Ground Capacity: 4,340
Seating Capacity: 504
Web site: www.gainsboroughtrinity.com

GENERAL INFORMATION
Supporters Club: G. Burton, c/o Club
Telephone Nº: (01427) 613688
Car Parking: Street parking and also in a Local Authority Car Park 150 yards from the ground towards the Town Centre
Coach Parking: Available by prior arrangement
Nearest Railway Station: Lea Road (2 miles)
Nearest Bus Station: Heaton Street (1 mile)
Club Shop: At the ground
Opening Times: Matchdays only
Telephone Nº: (01427) 611612
Police Telephone Nº: (01427) 810910

GROUND INFORMATION
Away Supporters' Entrances & Sections:
No usual segregation

ADMISSION INFO (2009/2010 PRICES)
Adult Standing: £10.00
Adult Seating: £11.00
Concessionary Standing: £6.00
Concessionary Seating: £7.00
Under-12s Standing/Seating: £2.00
Children Ages 12 to 16 Standing/Seating: £4.00
Programme Price: £1.50

DISABLED INFORMATION
Wheelchairs: Accommodated
Helpers: Please phone the club for information
Prices: Normal prices for the disabled. Free for helpers
Disabled Toilets: Available in new block adjacent to the Main Stand
Contact: (01427) 613295 (Bookings are not necessary)

Travelling Supporters' Information:
Routes: From the North, South and West: Exit the A1 at Blyth services taking the 1st left through to Bawtry. In Bawtry, turn right at the traffic lights onto the A631 straight through to Gainsborough (approx. 11 miles). Go over the bridge to the second set of traffic lights and turn left onto the A159 (Scunthorpe Road). Follow the main road past Tesco on the right through the traffic lights. The ground is situated on right approximately a third of a mile north of the Town Centre; From the East: Take the A631 into Gainsborough and turn right onto the A159. Then as above.

GLOUCESTER CITY FC

Founded: 1883
Former Names: Gloucester YMCA
Nickname: 'The Tigers'
Ground: Corinium Stadium, Kingshill Lane, Cirencester GL7 1HS
Record Attendance: 5,000 (1990 – Meadow Park)
Pitch Size: 112 × 72 yards

Colours: Shirts – Yellow & Black Stripes
Shorts – Black
Telephone Nº: 07813 931781
Fax Number: (01452) 530409
Ground Capacity: 4,000
Seating Capacity: 430
Web site: www.gloucestercityafc.com

GENERAL INFORMATION

Car Parking: At the ground
Coach Parking: At the ground
Nearest Railway Station: Kemble (3 miles)
Nearest Bus Station: Cirencester (1 mile)
Club Shop: At the ground
Opening Times: Matchdays only
Telephone Nº: (01452) 883904

GROUND INFORMATION

Away Supporters' Entrances & Sections:
No usual segregation

ADMISSION INFO (2009/2010 PRICES)

Adult Standing: £10.00
Adult Seating: £10.00
Concessionary Standing: £5.00
Concessionary Seating: £5.00
Note: Children aged ten and under are admitted free of charge
Programme Price: £1.50

DISABLED INFORMATION

Wheelchairs: Accommodated
Helpers: Admitted
Prices: Normal prices apply
Disabled Toilets: Available in the Clubhouse

Travelling Supporters' Information:
Routes: Leave the Cirencester Bypass (A46) at the Burford Road roundabout following signs for Stow. Turn right at the traffic lights then right again at the junction. Take the 1st left into Kingshill Lane and the ground is situated about ¼ mile on the right.

HARROGATE TOWN FC

Founded: 1919
Former Names: Harrogate FC and Harrogate Hotspurs FC
Nickname: 'Town'
Ground: CNG Stadium, Wetherby Road, Harrogate, HG2 7SA
Record Attendance: 4,280 (1950)

Pitch Size: 107 × 72 yards
Colours: Yellow and Black striped shirts, Black shorts
Telephone Nº: (01423) 880675 or 883671
Club Fax Number: (01423) 880675
Ground Capacity: 3,290
Seating Capacity: 502
Web site: www.harrogatetown.com

GENERAL INFORMATION

Supporters Club: c/o Phil Harrison, 14 Chatsworth Grove, Harrogate HG1 2AS
Telephone/Fax Nº: (01423) 525211
Car Parking: Hospital Car Park adjacent
Coach Parking: At the ground
Nearest Railway Station: Harrogate (¾ mile)
Nearest Bus Station: Harrogate
Club Shop: At the ground
Opening Times: Matchdays only
Telephone Nº: (01423) 325111
Police Telephone Nº: (01423) 505541

GROUND INFORMATION

Away Supporters' Entrances & Sections:
No usual segregation

ADMISSION INFO (2009/2010 PRICES)

Adult Standing: £11.00
Adult Seating: £12.00
Concessionary Standing: £7.00
Concessionary Seating: £8.00
Under-15s Standing: £2.00 (when with a paying adult)
Under-15s Seating: £3.00 (when with a paying adult)
Programme Price: £2.00

DISABLED INFORMATION

Wheelchairs: Accommodated at the front of the Main Stand
Helpers: Admitted
Prices: Free for the disabled when accompanied by a helper. Normal prices for helpers
Disabled Toilets: Available
Contact: (01423) 880675 (Bookings are not necessary)

Travelling Supporters' Information:
Routes: From the South: Take the A61 from Leeds and turn right at the roundabout onto the ring road (signposted York). After about 1¼ miles turn left at the next roundabout onto A661 Wetherby Road. The ground is situated ¾ mile on the right; From the West: Take the A59 straight into Wetherby Road from Empress Roundabout and the ground is on the left; From the East & North: Exit the A1(M) at Junction 47, take the A59 to Harrogate then follow the Southern bypass to Wetherby Road for the A661 Roundabout. Turn right towards Harrogate Town Centre and the ground is on the right after ¾ mile.

HINCKLEY UNITED FC

Founded: 1889
Former Names: Formed when Hinckley Athletic FC merged with Hinckley Town FC in 1997 (previously Westfield Rovers FC)
Nickname: 'The Knitters'
Ground: Greene King Stadium, Leicester Road, Hinckley LE10 3DR
Record Attendance: 3,231 (1st July 2008)

Pitch Size: 110 × 72 yards
Colours: Shirts are Red with Blue trim, Blue shorts
Telephone Nº: (01455) 840088
Contact Number: (01455) 840088
Ground Capacity: 4,329
Seating Capacity: 630
Web site: www.hinckleyunitedfc.co.uk

GENERAL INFORMATION

Supporters Club: c/o Club
Telephone Nº: (01455) 840088
Car Parking: At the ground (£2.00 charge per car)
Coach Parking: At the ground
Nearest Railway Station: Hinckley (2 miles)
Nearest Bus Station: Hinckley
Club Shop: At the ground
Opening Times: Matchdays only
Telephone Nº: (01455) 840088
Police Telephone Nº: (0116) 222-2222

GROUND INFORMATION

Away Supporters' Entrances & Sections:
West Stand and Terrace if required (no usual segregation)

ADMISSION INFO (2009/2010 PRICES)

Adult Standing: £9.00
Adult Seating: £10.00
Under-16s Standing: £3.00   (Under-12s admitted free)
Under-16s Seating: £4.00   (Under-12s admitted free)
Senior Citizen Standing: £6.00
Senior Citizen Seating: £7.00
Programme Price: £2.00

DISABLED INFORMATION

Wheelchairs: Accommodated
Helpers: Admitted
Prices: Normal prices apply
Disabled Toilets: Yes
Contact: (01455) 840088   (Bookings are not necessary)

Travelling Supporters' Information:
Routes: From the North-West: Take the A5 southbound and take the 1st exit at Dodwells roundabout onto the A47 towards Earl Shilton. Go straight on over 3 roundabouts then take the 3rd exit at the next roundabout onto the B4668. The entrance to the ground is on the right after 200 yards; From the South: Take the A5 northbound and upon reaching Dodwells roundabout take the 2nd exit onto the A47 towards East Shilton. Then as above; From the North-East: Take the M69, exit at Junction 2 and follow the B4669 towards Hinckley. After 2 miles (passing through 2 sets of traffic lights) bear right into Spa Lane then turn right at the next set of traffic lights onto the B4668 towards Earl Shilton. The Stadium is on the left after 1¾ miles.

HYDE UNITED FC

Founded: 1919
Former Names: Hyde FC (1885-1917)
Nickname: 'Tigers'
Ground: Tameside Stadium, Ewen Fields, Walker Lane, Hyde, Cheshire   SK14 2SB
Record Attendance: 9,500 (1952)
Pitch Size: 114 × 70 yards
Colours: Red shirts with White shorts

Telephone Nº: 0871 200-2116 (Matchdays) or 07778 792502 (Secretary)
Fax Number: 0871 200-2118 (Ground); (01270) 212473 (Secretary)
Ground Capacity: 4,250
Seating Capacity: 550
Web site: www.hydeunited.com

GENERAL INFORMATION

Supporters Club: Mark Dring, 16 Gainsborough Walk, Denton, Manchester   M34 6NS
Telephone Nº: (0161) 336-8076
Car Parking: 150 spaces available at the ground
Coach Parking: At the ground
Nearest Railway Station: Newton (¼ mile)
Nearest Bus Station: Hyde
Club Shop: At the ground
Opening Times: Matchdays only
Telephone Nº: 0871 200-2116
Police Telephone Nº: (0161) 330-8321

GROUND INFORMATION

Away Supporters' Entrances & Sections:
No usual segregation although it is used as required

ADMISSION INFO (2009/2010 PRICES)

Adult Standing: £10.00
Adult Seating: £12.00
Child Standing: £4.00
Child Seating: £6.00
Senior Citizen Standing: £4.00
Senior Citizen Seating: £6.00
Programme Price: £1.50

DISABLED INFORMATION

Wheelchairs: Accommodated in the disabled area
Helpers: Please phone the club for information
Prices: Please phone the club for information
Disabled Toilets: Yes
Contact: (01270) 212473   (Bookings are not necessary)

Travelling Supporters' Information:
Routes: Exit the M60 at Junction 24 and then exit the M67 at Junction 3 for Hyde. Turn right at the top of the slip road, left at the lights (Morrisons on the left). Turn right at the next set of lights into Lumn Road then turn left at the Give Way sign into Walker Lane. Take the 2nd Car Park entrance near the Leisure Pool and follow the road round for the Stadium.

ILKESTON TOWN FC

Founded: 1945
Former Names: None
Nickname: 'Robins'
Ground: New Manor Ground, Awsworth Road, Ilkeston, Derbyshire   DE7 8JF
Record Attendance: 2,538
Pitch Size: 113 × 74 yards

Colours: Red shirts and shorts
Telephone Nº: 07887 832125
Fax Number: –
Ground Capacity: 3,029
Seating Capacity: 550
Correspondence: K. Burnand, 2 Woodland Grove, Clowne, Chesterfield   S43 4AT
Web site: www.ilkeston-townfc.co.uk

GENERAL INFORMATION
Supporters Club: A. Middleton, c/o Club
Social Club Nº: (0115) 932-4094
Car Parking: At the ground
Coach Parking: At the ground
Nearest Railway Station: Derby (9 miles)
Nearest Bus Station: Ilkeston
Club Shop: At the ground
Opening Times: Matchdays only
Telephone Nº: (0115) 932-4094
Police Telephone Nº: (0115) 944-0100

GROUND INFORMATION
Away Supporters' Entrances & Sections:
No usual segregation, but can be used if necessary

ADMISSION INFO (2009/2010 PRICES)
Adult Standing: £9.00
Adult Seating: £10.00
Child Standing: £6.00
Child Seating: £7.00
Programme Price: £1.50

DISABLED INFORMATION
Wheelchairs: Accommodated
Helpers: Please phone the club for information
Prices: Please phone the club for information
Disabled Toilets: Yes
Are Bookings Necessary: No
Contact: (0115) 932-4094

Travelling Supporters' Information:
Routes: Exit the M1 at Junction 26 and take the A610 westwards for 2-3 miles. At the roundabout, turn left to Awsworth then at the next traffic island join the Awsworth Bypass following signs for Ilkeston A6096. After ½ mile turn right into Awsworth Road (signposted Cotmanhay) and the ground is ½ mile on the left.

NORTHWICH VICTORIA FC

Founded: 1874
Former Names: None
Nickname: 'The Vics' 'The Greens' 'The Trickies'
Ground: Marstons Arena, Wincham Avenue, Wincham, Northwich   CW9 6GB
Record Attendance: 3,216 (April 2006)
Pitch Size: 112 × 74 yards

Colours: Green and White shirts, White shorts
Office Telephone Nº: (01606) 815200
Fax Number: (01606) 43350
Ground Capacity: 5,046
Seating Capacity: 1,180
Web site: www.northwichvics.co.uk

GENERAL INFORMATION

Supporters Club: Mark Holman, c/o Club
Telephone Nº: (01606) 815200
Car Parking: Ample parking spaces available at the ground
Coach Parking: At the ground
Nearest Railway Station: Northwich (1½ miles)
Nearest Bus Station: Northwich (2½ miles)
Club Shop: At the ground
Opening Times: Weekdays & Matchdays 10.00am–4.00pm
Telephone Nº: (01606) 815200
Police Telephone Nº: (01606) 48000

GROUND INFORMATION

Away Supporters' Entrances & Sections: West Terrace

ADMISSION INFO (2009/2010 PRICES)

Adult Standing: £12.00
Adult Seating: £14.00
Senior Citizen Standing: £10.00
Senior Citizen Seating: £12.00
Under-16s Standing: £5.00
Under-16s Seating: £7.00
Under-12s Standing/Seating: £2.50
Programme Price: £2.00

DISABLED INFORMATION

Wheelchairs: 52 spaces are available in total
Helpers: Admitted
Prices: Normal prices for the disabled. Free for the helpers
Disabled Toilets: Yes
Contact: (01606) 815200   (Please phone to book)

Travelling Supporters' Information:
Routes: Exit the M6 at Junction 19 and take the A556 towards Northwich. After 3 miles turn right onto the A559 following signs for Warrington. Turn left after Marston opposite the Black Greyhound Inn then left into Wincham Avenue after 200 yards. Alternative Route: Exit the M56 at Junction 10 and take the A559 to the Black Greyhound Inn then turn right. Then as above

REDDITCH UNITED FC

Founded: 1891
Former Names: Redditch Town FC
Nickname: 'The Reds'
Ground: Valley Stadium, Bromsgrove Road, Redditch   B97 4RN
Record Attendance: 5,500 (vs Bromsgrove 1954/55)
Pitch Size: 110 × 72 yards

Colours: Red shirts, shorts and socks
Telephone Nº: (01527) 67450
Contact Nº: (01527) 67450
Fax Number: (01527) 67450
Ground Capacity: 5,000
Seating Capacity: 400
Web site: www.redditchunitedfc.co.uk

GENERAL INFORMATION

Supporters Club: c/o Club
Telephone Nº: (01527) 67450
Car Parking: At the ground
Coach Parking: At the ground
Nearest Railway Station: Redditch (¼ mile)
Nearest Bus Station: Redditch (¼ mile)
Club Shop: At the ground
Opening Times: Matchdays only

GROUND INFORMATION

Away Supporters' Entrances & Sections:
No segregation

ADMISSION INFO (2009/2010 PRICES)

Adult Standing: £8.00
Adult Seating: £9.00
Senior Citizen Standing: £5.00
Senior Citizen Seating: £6.00
Under-16s Standing/Seating: £1.00
Programme Price: £2.00

DISABLED INFORMATION

Wheelchairs: Accommodated
Helpers: Admitted
Prices: Normal prices apply to both helpers and disabled
Disabled Toilets: Available
Contact: (01527) 67450   (Bookings are not necessary)

Travelling Supporters' Information:
Routes: Exit the M42 at Junction 2 and follow the A441 towards Redditch. Take the 4th exit at the roundabout (signposted Batchley) and turn left at the traffic lights into Birmingham Road. Take the next right into Clive Road then left into Hewell Road. Continue to the T-junction and turn right, passing the Railway Station on the right. Continue through the traffic lights and the ground is situated on the right hand side after about ¼ mile.

SOLIHULL MOORS FC

Founded: 2007
Former Names: Formed by the merger of Solihull Borough FC and Moor Green FC in 2007
Nickname: 'The Moors'
Ground: Damson Park, Damson Parkway, Solihull, B91 2PP
Record Attendance: 2,000 (vs Birmingham City)

Pitch Size: 110 × 75 yards
Colours: White shirts with Black shorts
Telephone Nº: (0121) 705-6770
Fax Number: (0121) 711-4045
Ground Capacity: 3,050
Seating Capacity: 280
Web site: www.solihullmoorsfc.com

GENERAL INFORMATION

Supporters Club: Yes
Car Parking: At the ground
Coach Parking: At the ground
Nearest Railway Station: Birmingham International (2 miles)
Nearest Bus Station: Birmingham (5 miles)
Club Shop: At the ground
Opening Times: Matchdays only
Telephone Nº: (0121) 705-6770
Police Telephone Nº: (0121) 706-8111

GROUND INFORMATION

Away Supporters' Entrances & Sections:
No usual segregation

ADMISSION INFO (2009/2010 PRICES)

Adult Standing: £10.00
Adult Seating: £10.00
Senior Citizen/Junior Standing: £5.00
Senior Citizen/Junior Seating: £5.00
Note: Under-16s can purchase a season ticket for £30.00
Programme Price: £2.00

DISABLED INFORMATION

Wheelchairs: Spaces for 3 wheelchairs are available
Helpers: Admitted
Prices: Normal prices apply
Disabled Toilets: Available
Contact: (0121) 705-6770

Travelling Supporters' Information:
Routes: Exit the M42 at Junction 6 and take the A45 for 2 miles towards Birmingham. Turn left at the traffic lights near the Posthouse Hotel into Damson Parkway (signposted for Landrover/Damsonwood). Continue to the roundabout and come back along the other carriageway to the ground which is situated on the left after about 150 yards.

SOUTHPORT FC

Founded: 1881
Former Names: Southport Vulcan FC, Southport Central FC
Nickname: 'The Sandgrounders'
Ground: Haig Avenue, Southport, Merseyside, PR8 6JZ
Record Attendance: 20,010 (1932)
Pitch Size: 110 × 77 yards

Colours: Yellow shirts and shorts
Telephone Nº: (01704) 533422
Fax Number: (01704) 533455
Ground Capacity: 6,001
Seating Capacity: 1,640
Web site: www.southportfc.net

GENERAL INFORMATION
Supporters Club: Grandstand Club
Telephone Nº: (01704) 530182
Car Parking: Street parking
Coach Parking: Adjacent to the ground
Nearest Railway Station: Southport (1½ miles)
Nearest Bus Station: Southport Town Centre
Club Shop: At the ground
Opening Times: Matchdays from 1.30pm (from 6.30pm on evening matchdays)
Telephone Nº: (01704) 533422
Police Telephone Nº: (0151) 709-6010

GROUND INFORMATION
Away Supporters' Entrances & Sections:
Blowick End entrances

ADMISSION INFO (2009/2010 PRICES)
Adult Standing: £11.00
Adult Seating: £12.50
Child/Senior Citizen Standing: £7.50
Child/Senior Citizen Seating: £8.50
Programme Price: £2.50

DISABLED INFORMATION
Wheelchairs: Accommodated in front of the Grandstand
Helpers: Admitted
Prices: Concessionary prices charged for the disabled. Helpers are admitted free of charge
Disabled Toilets: Available at the Blowick End of the Grandstand
Contact: (01704) 533422 (Bookings are not necessary)

Travelling Supporters' Information:
Routes: Exit the M58 at Junction 3 and take the A570 to Southport. At the major roundabout (McDonalds/Tesco) go straight on into Scarisbrick New Road, pass over the brook and turn right into Haig Avenue at the traffic lights. The ground is then on the right-hand side.

STAFFORD RANGERS FC

Founded: 1876
Former Names: None
Nickname: 'The Boro'
Ground: Marston Road, Stafford   ST16 3BX
Record Attendance: 8,523 (4th January 1975)
Pitch Size: 112 × 75 yards

Colours: Black and White striped shirts, Black shorts
Telephone Nº: (01785) 602430
Social Club Nº: (01785) 602432
Ground Capacity: 4,250
Seating Capacity: 2,157
Web site: www.staffordrangers.co.uk

GENERAL INFORMATION

Supporters Club: c/o Social Club
Telephone Nº: (01785) 602432
Car Parking: At the ground
Coach Parking: Astonfields Road
Nearest Railway Station: Stafford (1½ miles)
Nearest Bus Station: Stafford
Club Shop: At the ground
Opening Times: Matchdays only
Telephone Nº: (01785) 602430
Police Telephone Nº: (01785) 258151

GROUND INFORMATION

Away Supporters' Entrances & Sections:
Lotus End

ADMISSION INFO (2009/2010 PRICES)

Adult Standing: £11.00
Adult Seating: £13.00
Concessionary Standing: £7.00
Concessionary Seating: £9.00
Children under the age of 12 are admitted free of charge
when accompanying a paying adult
Programme Price: £2.50

DISABLED INFORMATION

Wheelchairs: Accommodated at Marston Road End
Helpers: Admitted
Prices: Concessionary prices for the disabled. Normal prices
for helpers
Disabled Toilets: Available
Contact: (01785) 602430   (Bookings are not necessary)

Travelling Supporters' Information:
Routes: Exit the M6 at Junction 14 and take the slip road signposted 'Stone/Stafford'. Continue to traffic island and go straight across then take the 3rd exit on the right into Common Road, signposted 'Common Road/Aston Fields Industrial Estate'. Follow the road to the bridge and bear left over the bridge. The ground is on the right.

STALYBRIDGE CELTIC FC

Founded: 1909
Former Names: None
Nickname: 'Celtic'
Ground: Bower Fold, Mottram Road, Stalybridge, Cheshire   SK15 2RT
Record Attendance: 9,753 (1922/23)
Pitch Size: 109 × 70 yards

Colours: Blue shirts, White shorts and Blue socks
Telephone N°: (0161) 338-2828
Daytime Phone N°: (0161) 338-2828
Fax Number: (0161) 338-8256
Ground Capacity: 6,108
Seating Capacity: 1,155
Web site: www.stalybridgeceltic.co.uk

GENERAL INFORMATION

Supporters Club: Bob Rhodes, c/o Club
Telephone N°: (01457) 764044
Car Parking: At the ground
Coach Parking: At the ground
Nearest Railway Station: Stalybridge (1 mile)
Nearest Bus Station: Stalybridge town centre
Club Shop: At the ground
Opening Times: Matchdays only
Telephone N°: (0161) 338-2828
Police Telephone N°: (0161) 872-5050

GROUND INFORMATION

Away Supporters' Entrances & Sections:
Lockwood & Greenwood Stand

ADMISSION INFO (2009/2010 PRICES)

Adult Standing: £10.00
Adult Seating: £10.00
Under-14s Standing/Seating: Free of charge
Concessionary Standing: £6.00
Concessionary Seating: £6.00
Programme Price: £2.00

DISABLED INFORMATION

Wheelchairs: 20 spaces available each for home and away fans at the side of the Stepan Stand. A further 9 spaces available in the new Lord Tom Pendry Stand
Helpers: Please phone the club for information
Prices: Please phone the club for information
Disabled Toilets: Available at the rear of the Stepan Stand and at the side of the Lord Tom Pendry Stand
Contact: (0161) 338-2828   (Bookings are necessary)

Travelling Supporters' Information:
Routes: From the Midlands and South: Take the M6, M56, M60 and M67, leaving at the end of the motorway. Go across the roundabout to the traffic lights and turn left. The ground is approximately 2 miles on the left before the Hare & Hounds pub; From the North: Exit the M62 at Junction 18 onto the M60 singposted for Ashton-under-Lyne. Follow the M60 to Junction 24 and join the M67, then as from the Midlands and South.

VAUXHALL MOTORS FC

Founded: 1963
Former Names: Vauxhall GM FC
Nickname: 'Motormen'
Ground: Motassist Arena, Hooton, Ellesmere Port, Cheshire   CH66 1NJ
Record Attendance: 1,500 (1987)
Pitch Size: 117 × 78 yards
Colours: White shirts with Dark Blue shorts

Telephone Nº: (0151) 328-1114 (Ground)
Ground Capacity: 3,306
Seating Capacity: 266
Contact: Carole Paisey, 31 South Road, West Kirby, Wirral   CH48 3HG
Contact Phone and Fax Nº: (0151) 625-6936
Web site: www.vmfc.com
E-mail: office@vmfc.com

GENERAL INFORMATION
Supporters Club: At the ground
Telephone/Fax Nº: (0151) 328-1114
Car Parking: At the ground
Coach Parking: At the ground
Nearest Railway Station: Overpool
Nearest Bus Station: Ellesmere Port
Club Shop: At the ground
Opening Times: Matchdays only
Telephone Nº: –

GROUND INFORMATION
Away Supporters' Entrances & Sections:
No usual segregation

ADMISSION INFO (2009/2010 PRICES)
Adult Standing/Seating: £8.00
Child Standing/Seating: £3.00
Senior Citizen Standing/Seating: £5.00
Programme Price: £2.00

DISABLED INFORMATION
Wheelchairs: Accommodated as necessary
Helpers: Admitted
Prices: Normal prices for the disabled. Free for carers
Disabled Toilets: Available
Contact: –   (Bookings are not necessary)

Travelling Supporters' Information:
Routes: Exit the M53 at Junction 5 and take the A41 towards Chester. Turn left at the first set of traffic lights into Hooton Green. Turn left at the first T-junction then right at the next T-junction into Rivacre Road. The ground is situated 250 yards on the right.

WORKINGTON AFC

Founded: 1884 (Reformed 1921)
Former Names: None
Nickname: 'Reds'
Ground: Borough Park, Workington   CA14 2DT
Record Attendance: 21,000 (vs Manchester United)
Pitch Size: 110 × 71 yards

Colours: Red shirts and shorts
Telephone Nº: (01900) 602871
Fax Number: (01900) 67432
Ground Capacity: 3,100
Seating Capacity: 500
Web site: www.workingtonafc.com

GENERAL INFORMATION
Supporters Club: Yes
Car Parking: Car Park next to the ground
Coach Parking: At the ground
Nearest Railway Station: Workington (¼ mile)
Nearest Bus Station: Workington (½ mile)
Club Shop: At the ground
Opening Times: Matchdays only
Telephone Nº: (01946) 832710

GROUND INFORMATION
Away Supporters' Entrances & Sections:
No usual segregation

ADMISSION INFO (2009/2010 PRICES)
Adult Standing: £10.00
Adult Seating: £10.00
Senior Citizen/Junior/Student Standing: £5.00
Senior Citizen/Junior/Student Seating: £5.00
Note: Under-5s are admitted free of charge
Programme Price: £1.80

DISABLED INFORMATION
Wheelchairs: Accommodated
Helpers: Admitted
Prices: Normal prices apply
Disabled Toilets: Available
Contact: (01900) 602871   (Bookings are not necessary)

Travelling Supporters' Information:
Routes: Exit the M6 at Junction 40 and take the A66 towards Keswick and Workington. Upon reaching Workington, continue until you reach the traffic lights at a T-junction. Turn right here onto the A596 for Maryport. After approximately ½ mile you will see the ground floodlights on the opposite site of the river (to the left). Continue along the A596, pass under the bridge taking the next right signposted for the Stadium. The ground is then on the left hand side opposite the Tesco superstore.

THE FOOTBALL CONFERENCE BLUE SQUARE SOUTH

Address

Third Floor, Wellington House,
31-34 Waterloo Street, Birmingham   B2 5TJ

Phone (0121) 214-1950

Web site   www.footballconference.co.uk

Clubs for the 2009/2010 Season

Basingstoke Town FC .... Page 54
Bath City FC .... Page 55
Bishop's Stortford FC .... Page 56
Braintree Town FC .... Page 57
Bromley FC .... Page 58
Chelmsford City FC .... Page 59
Dorchester Town FC.. Page 60
Dover Athletic FC .... Page 61
Eastleigh FC .... Page 62
Hampton & Richmond Borough FC .... Page 63
Havant & Waterlooville FC .... Page 64
Lewes FC .... Page 65
Maidenhead United FC .... Page 66
Newport County AFC .... Page 67
St. Albans City FC .... Page 68
Staines Town FC .... Page 69
Thurrock FC .... Page 70
Welling United FC .... Page 71
Weston-Super-Mare FC .... Page 72
Weymouth FC... Page 73
Woking FC .... Page 74
Worcester City FC... Page 75

BASINGSTOKE TOWN FC

Founded: 1896
Former Names: None
Nickname: 'Dragons'
Ground: The Camrose Ground, Western Way, Basingstoke, Hants. RG22 6EZ
Record Attendance: 5,085 (25th November 1997)
Pitch Size: 110 × 70 yards

Colours: Yellow and Blue shirts with Blue shorts
Telephone Nº: (01256) 327575
Fax Number: (01256) 869997
Social Club Nº: (01256) 464353
Ground Capacity: 6,000
Seating Capacity: 650
Web site: www.basingstoketown.net

GENERAL INFORMATION

Supporters Club: c/o Club
Telephone Nº: (01256) 327575
Car Parking: 600 spaces available at the ground
Coach Parking: Ample room available at ground
Nearest Railway Station: Basingstoke
Nearest Bus Station: Basingstoke Town Centre (2 miles)
Club Shop: The Camrose Shop
Opening Times: Matchdays only
Telephone Nº: (01256) 327575
Police Telephone Nº: (01256) 473111

GROUND INFORMATION

Away Supporters' Entrances & Sections:
No usual segregation

ADMISSION INFO (2009/2010 PRICES)

Adult Standing: £10.00
Adult Seating: £11.00
Concessionary Standing: £6.00
Concessionary Seating: £7.00
Under-16s Standing: £3.00
Under-16s Seating: £4.00
Programme Price: £2.00

DISABLED INFORMATION

Wheelchairs: 6 spaces are available under cover
Helpers: Admitted
Prices: Normal prices for the disabled. Free for helpers
Disabled Toilets: Yes
Contact: (01256) 327575 (Bookings are not necessary)

Travelling Supporters' Information:
Routes: Exit the M3 at Junction 6 and take the 1st left at the Black Dam roundabout. At the next roundabout take the 2nd exit, then the 1st exit at the following roundabout and the 5th exit at the next roundabout. This takes you into Western Way and the ground is 50 yards on the right.

BATH CITY FC

Founded: 1889
Former Names: Bath AFC, Bath Railway FC and Bath Amateurs FC
Nickname: 'The Romans'
Ground: Twerton Park, Bath BA2 1DB
Record Attendance: 18,020 (1960)
Pitch Size: 110 × 76 yards

Colours: Black and White striped shirts, Black shorts
Telephone Nº: (01225) 423087/313247
Fax Number: (01225) 481391
Ground Capacity: 8,840
Seating Capacity: 1,026
Web site: www.bathcityfc.com

GENERAL INFORMATION
Supporters Club: Martin Brush, c/o Club
Telephone Nº: (01225) 423087
Car Parking: 150 spaces available at the ground
Coach Parking: Available at the ground
Nearest Railway Station: Bath Spa (1½ miles)
Nearest Bus Station: Avon Street, Bath
Club Shop: Yes – contact Martin Brush, c/o Club
Opening Times: Matchdays and office hours
Telephone Nº: (01225) 423087

GROUND INFORMATION
Away Supporters' Entrances & Sections:
No usual segregation

ADMISSION INFO (2009/2010 PRICES)
Adult Standing: £10.00
Adult Seating: £12.00
Senior Citizen Standing: £7.00
Senior Citizen Seating: £8.00
Under-16s Standing: £4.00
Under-16s Seating: £5.00
Programme Price: £1.50

DISABLED INFORMATION
Wheelchairs: 10 spaces available each for home and away fans in front of the Family Stand
Helpers: Admitted
Prices: £7.00 for the disabled. Free entrance for helpers
Disabled Toilets: Available behind the Family Stand
Contact: (01225) 423087   (Bookings are not necessary)

Travelling Supporters' Information:
Route: As a recommendation, avoid exiting the M4 at Junction 18 as the road from takes you through Bath City Centre. Instead, exit the M4 at Junction 19 onto the M32. Turn off the M32 at Junction 1 and follow the A4174 Bristol Ring Road south then join the A4 for Bath. On the A4, after passing through Saltford you will reach a roundabout shortly before entering Bath. Take the 2nd exit at this roundabout then follow the road before turning left into Newton Road at the bottom of the steep hill. The ground is then on the right hand side of the road.

BISHOP'S STORTFORD FC |

Founded: 1874
Former Names: None
Nickname: 'Blues' 'Bishops'
Ground: Woodside Park, Dunmow Road,
Bishop's Stortford   CM23 5RG
Record Attendance: 3,555 (2000)
Pitch Size: 110 × 70 yards

Colours: Blue and White shirts with Blue shorts
Telephone Nº: (08700) 339930
Fax Number: (08700) 339931
Ground Capacity: 4,000
Seating Capacity: 500
Web site: www.bsfc.co.uk

GENERAL INFORMATION

Supporters Club: None
Car Parking: 150 spaces available at the ground
Coach Parking: At the ground
Nearest Railway Station: Bishop's Stortford
Nearest Bus Station: Bishop's Stortford
Club Shop: At the ground
Opening Times: Matchdays only 1.30pm to 5.00pm
Telephone Nº: (08700) 339930
Police Telephone Nº: –

GROUND INFORMATION

Away Supporters' Entrances & Sections:
No usual segregation

ADMISSION INFO (2009/2010 PRICES)

Adult Standing/Seating: £10.00
Concessionary Standing/Seating: £6.00
Child Standing/Seating: £4.00
Note: Under-12s are admitted free of charge when
accompanied by a paying adult.
Programme Price: £2.00

DISABLED INFORMATION

Wheelchairs: Accommodated in the disabled section
Helpers: Admitted
Prices: Free of charge for the disabled and helpers
Disabled Toilets: Yes
Contact: (08700) 339930   (Bookings are not necessary)

Travelling Supporters' Information:
Routes: Exit the M11 at junction 8 and take the A1250 towards Bishop Stortford. Turn left at the first roundabout and the
ground is first right opposite the Golf Club (the entrance is between Industrial Units).

BRAINTREE TOWN FC

Founded: 1898
Former Names: Manor Works FC, Crittall Athletic FC, Braintree & Crittall Athletic FC and Braintree FC
Nickname: 'The Iron'
Ground: Cressing Road Stadium, Clockhouse Way, Braintree, Essex   CM7 6RD
Record Attendance: 4,000 (May 1952)
Pitch Size: 111 × 78 yards

Ground Capacity: 4,157
Seating Capacity: 556
Colours: Yellow shirts and shorts
Telephone Nº: (01376) 345617
Fax Number: (01376) 330976
Correspondence Address: Tom Woodley, 19A Bailey Bridge Road, Braintree   CM7 5TT
Contact Telephone Nº: (01376) 326234
Web site: www.braintreetownfc.org.uk

GENERAL INFORMATION

Supporters Club: c/o Club
Telephone Nº: (01376) 345617
Car Parking: At the ground
Coach Parking: At the ground
Nearest Railway Station: Braintree (1 mile)
Nearest Bus Station: Braintree
Club Shop: At the ground
Opening Times: Matchdays only
Telephone Nº: (01376) 345617

GROUND INFORMATION

Away Supporters' Entrances & Sections: Gates 1-4

ADMISSION INFO (2009/2010 PRICES)

Adult Standing: £10.00
Adult Seating: £12.00
Child Standing: £5.00
Child Seating: £7.00
Programme Price: £2.00

DISABLED INFORMATION

Wheelchairs: Accommodated
Helpers: Admitted
Prices: Normal prices apply
Disabled Toilets: Available
Contact: (01376) 345617

Travelling Supporters' Information:
Routes: Exit the A120 Braintree Bypass at the McDonald's roundabout following signs for East Braintree Industrial Estate. The floodlights at the ground are visible on the left ½ mile into town. Turn left into Clockhouse Way then left again for the ground.

BROMLEY FC

THE JOHN FIORINI STAND

Founded: 1892
Former Names: None
Nickname: 'Lillywhites'
Ground: The Stadium, Hayes Lane, Bromley, Kent, BR2 9EF
Record Attendance: 12,000 (24th September 1949)
Pitch Size: 112 × 72 yards

Colours: White shirts with Black shorts
Telephone Nº: (020) 8460-5291
Fax Number: –
Ground Capacity: 3,300
Seating Capacity: 1,300
Web site: www.bromleyfc.net

GENERAL INFORMATION

Car Parking: 300 spaces available at the ground
Coach Parking: At the ground
Nearest Railway Station: Bromley South (1 mile)
Nearest Bus Station: High Street, Bromley
Club Shop: At the ground
Opening Times: Matchdays only
Telephone Nº: (020) 8460-5291

GROUND INFORMATION

Away Supporters' Entrances & Sections:
No usual segregation

ADMISSION INFO (2009/2010 PRICES)

Adult Standing: £10.00
Adult Seating: £10.00
Child/Senior Citizen Standing: £5.00
Child/Senior Citizen Seating: £5.00
Note: Under-5s are admitted free of charge
Programme Price: £2.00

DISABLED INFORMATION

Wheelchairs: Accommodated
Helpers: Admitted
Prices: Please phone the club for information
Disabled Toilets: Yes
Contact: (0181) 460-5291 (Bookings are necessary)

Travelling Supporters' Information:
Routes: Exit the M25 at Junction 4 and follow the A21 for Bromley and London for approximately 4 miles before forking left onto the A232 signposted for Croydon/Sutton. At the second set of traffic lights turn right into Baston Road (B265) and follow for approximately 2 miles as it becomes Hayes Street and then Hayes Lane. The ground is on the right just after a mini-roundabout.

CHELMSFORD CITY FC

Founded: 1938	**Colours**: Claret and White shirts and shorts
Former Names: Chelmsford FC	**Telephone Nº**: (01245) 290959
Nickname: 'City' or 'Clarets'	**Fax Number**: –
Ground: Chelmsford Athletics and Sport Centre, Salerno Way, Chelmsford CM1 2EH	**Ground Capacity**: 3,000
	Seating Capacity: 1,400
Record Attendance: 16,807 (at previous ground)	**Web site**: www.chelmsfordcityfc.com
Pitch Size: 109 × 70 yards	

GENERAL INFORMATION

Car Parking: Limited space at ground and street parking
Coach Parking: Two spaces available at the ground subject to advance notice
Nearest Railway Station: Chelmsford (2 miles)
Nearest Bus Station: Chelmsford (2 miles)
Club Shop: At the ground within the Clubhouse
Opening Times: Matchdays only at present
Telephone Nº: (01245) 290959
Police Telephone Nº: (01245) 491212

GROUND INFORMATION

Away Supporters' Entrances & Sections:
No usual segregation

ADMISSION INFO (2009/2010 PRICES)

Adult Standing: £10.00
Adult Seating: £11.00
Child Standing: £3.00
Child Seating: £4.00
Concessionary Standing: £6.50
Concessionary Seating: £7.50
Programme Price: £2.00

DISABLED INFORMATION

Wheelchairs: Spaces for 11 wheelchairs available
Helpers: Admitted
Prices: Same prices as standing admission
Disabled Toilets: Available
Contact: (01245) 290959   (Bookings are necessary)

Travelling Supporters' Information:
Route: The ground is situated next to the only set of high rise flats in Chelmsford which can therefore be used as a landmark. From the A12 from London: Exit the A12 at Junction 15 signposted for Chelmsford/Harlow/A414 and head towards Chelmsford along the dual-carriageway. At the third roundabout, immediately after passing the 'Superbowl' on the left, take the first exit into Westway, signposted for the Crematorium and Widford Industrial Estate. Continue along Westway which becomes Waterhouse Lane after the second set of traffic lights. At the next set of lights (at the gyratory system) take the first exit into Rainsford Road, signposted for Sawbridgeworth A1060. Continue along Rainsford Road then turn right into Chignal Road at the second set of traffic lights. Turn right again into Melbourne Avenue and Salerno Way is on the left at the end of the football pitches.

DORCHESTER TOWN FC

Founded: 1880
Former Names: None
Nickname: 'The Magpies'
Ground: The Jewson Stadium, Weymouth Avenue, Dorchester, Dorset DT1 2RY
Record Attendance: 4,159 (1st January 1999)
Pitch Size: 110 × 80 yards

Colours: White shirts with Black shorts and socks
Telephone N°: (01305) 262451
Daytime N°: (01305) 262451
Fax Number: (01305) 267623
Ground Capacity: 5,009
Seating Capacity: 710
Web Site: www.dorchestertownfc.co.uk

GENERAL INFORMATION

Supporters Club: H.G. Gill, 39 Thatcham Park, Yeovil, Somerset
Telephone N°: (01935) 422536
Car Parking: 350 spaces available at the ground (£1.00 fee)
Coach Parking: At the ground
Nearest Railway Station: Dorchester South and West (both 1 mile)
Nearest Bus Station: Nearby
Club Shop: At the ground
Opening Times: During 1st team matchdays only
Telephone N°: (01305) 262451
Police Telephone N°: (01305) 251212

GROUND INFORMATION

Away Supporters' Entrances & Sections:
Main Stand side when segregated (not usual)

ADMISSION INFO (2009/2010 PRICES)

Adult Standing: £9.00
Adult Seating: £10.00
Senior Citizen/Child Standing: £5.50
Senior Citizen/Child Seating: £6.50
Under-16s: £2.50 when accompanied by a paying adult
Programme Price: £2.00

DISABLED INFORMATION

Wheelchairs: 10 spaces available each for home and away fans at the North West End of the terracing
Helpers: Admitted
Prices: Normal prices apply
Disabled Toilets: 2 available near the disabled area
Contact: (01305) 262451   (Bookings are not necessary)

Travelling Supporters' Information:
Routes: Take the Dorchester Bypass (A35) from all directions. The ground is on the South side of town, adjacent to a roundabout at the intersection with the A354 to Weymouth. Alternatively, take Weymouth signs from Dorchester Town Centre for 1½ miles.

DOVER ATHLETIC FC

Founded: 1983
Former Names: None
Nickname: 'The Whites'
Ground: Crabble Athletic Ground, Lewisham Road, River, Dover CT17 0JB
Record Attendance: 4,186 (2002)
Pitch Size: 111 × 73 yards

Colours: White shirts with Black shorts
Telephone Nº: (01304) 822373
Fax Number: (01304) 821383
Ground Capacity: 6,500
Seating Capacity: 1,000
Web site: www.dover-athletic.co.uk

GENERAL INFORMATION

Supporters Trust: Simon Harris, c/o Club
Telephone Nº: –
Car Parking: Street parking
Coach Parking: Street parking
Nearest Railway Station: Kearsney (1 mile)
Nearest Bus Station: Pencester Road, Dover (1½ miles)
Club Shop: At the ground
Opening Times: Saturdays 9.00am to 12.00pm
Telephone Nº: (01304) 822373
Police Telephone Nº: (01304) 240055

GROUND INFORMATION

Away Supporters' Entrances & Sections:
Segregation only used when required

ADMISSION INFO (2009/2010 PRICES)

Adult Standing: £10.00
Adult Seating: £11.50
Senior Citizen Standing: £7.00
Child Standing/Seating: £5.00   (Under-11s £2.00)
Senior Citizen Standing/Seating: £8.50
Programme Price: £2.50

DISABLED INFORMATION

Wheelchairs: Approximately 20 spaces are available in front of the Family Stand
Helpers: Please phone the club for information
Prices: Please phone the club for information
Disabled Toilets: None
Contact: – (Bookings are not necessary)

Travelling Supporters' Information:
Routes: Take the A2 to the Whitfield roundabout and take the 4th exit. Travel down the hill to the mini-roundabout then turn left and follow the road for 1 mile to the traffic lights on the hill. Turn sharp right and pass under the railway bridge – the ground is on the left after 300 yards.

EASTLEIGH FC

Photo courtesy of the Southern Daily Echo

Founded: 1946
Former Names: Swaythling Athletic FC and Swaythling FC
Nickname: 'The Spitfires'
Ground: Silverlake Stadium, Ten Acres, Stoneham Lane, Eastleigh   SO50 9HT
Record Attendance: 3,104 (2006)
Pitch Size: 112 × 74 yards

Colours: White shirts with Royal Blue shorts
Telephone Nº: (023) 8061-3361
Fax Number: (023) 8061-2379
Ground Capacity: 3,000
Seating Capacity: 512
Web site: www.eastleigh-fc.co.uk
e-mail: commercial@eastleigh-fc.co.uk

GENERAL INFORMATION
Car Parking: Spaces for 450 cars available (hard standing)
Coach Parking: At the ground
Nearest Railway Station: Southampton Parkway (¾ mile)
Nearest Bus Station: Eastleigh (2 miles)
Club Shop: At the ground
Opening Times: Matchdays and during functions only

GROUND INFORMATION
Away Supporters' Entrances & Sections:
No usual segregation

ADMISSION INFO (2009/2010 PRICES)
Adult Standing/Seating: £10.00
Senior Citizen Standing/Seating: £6.00
Under-16s Standing/Seating: £3.00
Under-12s: Free of charge
Programme Price: £2.00

DISABLED INFORMATION
Wheelchairs: Accommodated
Helpers: Admitted
Prices: Normal prices apply
Disabled Toilets: Available
Contact: (023) 8061-3361   (Bookings are not necessary)

Travelling Supporters' Information:
Routes: Exit the M27 at Junction 5 (signposted for Southampton Airport) and take the A335 (Stoneham Way) towards Southampton. After ½ mile, turn right at the traffic lights into Bassett Green Road. Turn right at the next set of traffic lights into Stoneham Lane and the ground is on the right after ¾ mile.

HAMPTON & RICHMOND BOROUGH FC

Founded: 1921
Former Names: Hampton FC
Nickname: 'Beavers'
Ground: Beveree Stadium, Beaver Close,
off Station Road, Hampton, Middlesex TW12 2BX
Record Attendance: 3,500 vs West Ham United
Pitch Size: 113 × 71 yards

Colours: Red shirts with Blue flash, Red shorts
Matchday Phone Nº: (020) 8979-2456
Fax Number: (020) 8979-2456
Ground Capacity: 3,500
Seating Capacity: 300
Web site: www.hamptonfc.net

GENERAL INFORMATION

Supporters Club: Yes
Telephone Nº: (020) 8979-2456
Car Parking: At the ground and street parking
Coach Parking: Contact the Club for information
Nearest Railway Station: Hampton
Nearest Bus Station: Hounslow/Kingston/Fulwell
Club Shop: At the ground
Opening Times: Matchdays only
Telephone Nº: –
Police Telephone Nº: (020) 8577-1212

GROUND INFORMATION

Away Supporters' Entrances & Sections:
No usual segregation

ADMISSION INFO (2009/2010 PRICES)

Adult Standing: £11.00
Adult Seating: £11.00
Senior Citizen/Concessionary Standing: £5.00
Senior Citizen/Concessionary Seating: £5.00
Junior Standing: £5.00 (Ages 4-16)
Junior Seating: £5.00 (Ages 4-16)
Programme Price: £2.50

DISABLED INFORMATION

Wheelchairs: Accommodated
Helpers: Admitted
Prices: Normal prices apply
Disabled Toilets: Available
Contact: (020) 8979-2456 (Bookings are not necessary)

Travelling Supporters' Information:
Routes: From the South: Exit the M3 at Junction 1 and follow the A308 (signposted Kingston). Turn 1st left after Kempton Park into Percy Road. Turn right at the level crossing into Station Road then left into Beaver Close for the ground; From the North: Take the A305 from Twickenham then turn left onto the A311. Pass through Hampton Hill onto Hampton High Street. Turn right at the White Hart pub (just before the junction with the A308), then right into Station Road and right again into Beaver Close.

HAVANT & WATERLOOVILLE FC

Founded: 1998
Former Names: Formed by the amalgamation of Waterlooville FC and Havant Town FC
Nickname: 'The Hawks'
Ground: Westleigh Park, Martin Road, Havant, PO9 5TH
Record Attendance: 5,757 (2006/07)
Pitch Size: 112 × 76 yards

Colours: White shirts and shorts
Telephone Nº: (023) 9278-7822 (Ground)
Fax Number: (023) 9226-2367
Ground Capacity: 5,800
Seating Capacity: 562
Web site: www.havantandwaterlooville.net

GENERAL INFORMATION

Supporters Club: None, but large Social Club
Telephone Nº: (023) 9278-7855
Car Parking: Space for 750 cars at the ground
Coach Parking: At the ground
Nearest Railway Station: Havant (1 mile)
Nearest Bus Station: Town Centre (1½ miles)
Club Shop: At the ground
Opening Times: Daily
Telephone Nº: (023) 9278-7822
Police Telephone Nº: (0845) 454545

GROUND INFORMATION

Away Supporters' Entrances & Sections: Martin Road End

ADMISSION INFO (2009/2010 PRICES)

Adult Standing: £10.00
Adult Seating: £10.00
Senior Citizen Standing/Seating: £6.00
Note: When accompanied by a paying adult, children under the age of 11 are admitted free of charge
Programme Price: £2.00

DISABLED INFORMATION

Wheelchairs: 12 spaces available in the Main Stand
Helpers: Admitted
Prices: Normal prices for disabled fans. Free for helpers
Disabled Toilets: Two available
Contact: (023) 9226-7276   (Bookings are necessary)

Travelling Supporters' Information:
Routes: From London or the North take the A27 from Chichester and exit at the B2149 turn-off for Havant. Take the 2nd exit off the dual carriageway into Bartons Road and then the 1st right into Martin Road for the ground; From the West: Take the M27 then the A27 to the Petersfield exit. Then as above.

LEWES FC

Founded: 1885
Former Names: None
Nickname: 'Rooks'
Ground: The Dripping Pan, Mountfield Road,
Lewes BN7 2XD
Record Attendance: 2,500 (vs Newhaven 26/12/47)
Pitch Size: 109 × 74 yards

Colours: Red & Black striped shirts with Black shorts
Telephone Nº: (01273) 472100
Fax Number: (01273) 483210
Ground Capacity: 3,000
Seating Capacity: 500
Web site: www.lewesfc.com

GENERAL INFORMATION
Supporters Club: c/o Club
Telephone Nº: (01273) 472100
Car Parking: At the ground
Coach Parking: At Lewes Railway Station (adjacent)
Nearest Railway Station: Lewes (adjacent)
Nearest Bus Station: Lewes (½ mile)
Club Shop: At the ground.
Opening Times: Matchdays only

GROUND INFORMATION
Away Supporters' Entrances & Sections:
No usual segregation – otherwise as directed by stewards

ADMISSION INFO (2009/2010 PRICES)
Adult Standing: £10.00
Adult Seating: £10.00
Junior (Under-14s) Standing: £2.00
Junior (Under-14s) Seating: £2.00
Senior Citizen/Under-16s Standing: £5.00
Senior Citizen/Under-16s Seating: £5.00
Programme Price: £2.00

DISABLED INFORMATION
Wheelchairs: Accommodated
Helpers: Admitted
Prices: Normal prices apply for the disabled and helpers
Disabled Toilets: Available
Contact: (01273) 472100

Travelling Supporters' Information:
Routes: From the North: Take the A26 or the A275 to Lewes and follow signs for the Railway Station. Pass the station on the left and take the next left. The ground is adjacent; From the South and West: Take the A27 to the A26 for the Town Centre. Then as above.

MAIDENHEAD UNITED FC

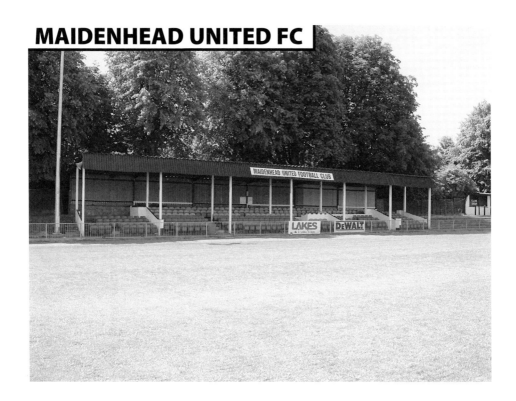

Founded: 1870
Former Names: None
Nickname: 'Magpies'
Ground: York Road, Maidenhead, Berks. SL6 1SF
Record Attendance: 7,920 (1936)
Pitch Size: 110 × 75 yards

Colours: Black and White striped shirts, Black shorts
Telephone Nº: (01628) 636314 (Club)
Contact Number: (01628) 636078
Ground Capacity: 4,500
Seating Capacity: 400
Web site: www.maidenheadunitedfc.co.uk

GENERAL INFORMATION
Supporters Club: c/o Club
Telephone Nº: (01628) 636314
Car Parking: Street parking
Coach Parking: Street parking
Nearest Railway Station: Maidenhead (¼ mile)
Nearest Bus Station: Maidenhead
Club Shop: At the ground
Opening Times: Matchdays only
Telephone Nº: (01628) 624739
Police Telephone Nº: –

GROUND INFORMATION
Away Supporters' Entrances & Sections:
No usual segregation

ADMISSION INFO (2009/2010 PRICES)
Adult Standing: £10.00
Adult Seating: £10.00
Concessionary Standing and Seating: £6.00
Child Standing and Seating: £2.00 (Under-16s)
Programme Price: £1.00

DISABLED INFORMATION
Wheelchairs: Accommodated
Helpers: Admitted
Prices: Normal prices for the disabled. Free for helpers
Disabled Toilets: Available
Contact: (01628) 636078   (Bookings are not necessary)

Travelling Supporters' Information:
Routes: Exit M4 at Junction 7 and take the A4 to Maidenhead. Cross the River Thames bridge and turn left at the 2nd roundabout passing through the traffic lights. York Road is first right and the ground is approximately 300 yards along on the left.

NEWPORT COUNTY AFC

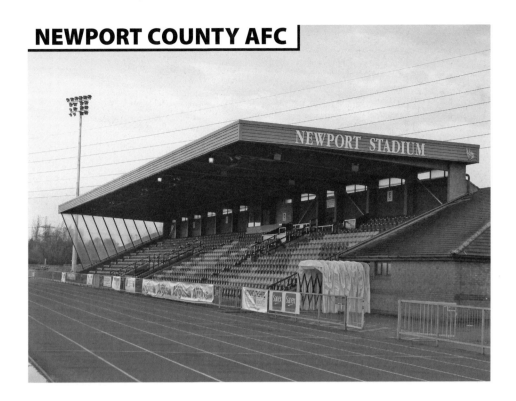

Founded: 1989
Former Names: Newport AFC
Nickname: 'The Exiles'
Ground: Newport Stadium, Stadium Way, Newport International Sports Village, Newport NP19 4PT
Record Attendance: 4,616 (11th November 2006)
Pitch Size: 112 × 72 yards

Colours: Amber shirts with Black shorts
Telephone Nº: (01633) 662262
Fax Number: (01633) 666107
Ground Capacity: 4,300
Seating Capacity: 1,236
Web site: www.newport-county.co.uk

GENERAL INFORMATION

Supporters Club: Bob Herrin, c/o Club
Telephone Nº: (01633) 274440
Car Parking: Space for 500 cars at the ground
Coach Parking: At the ground
Nearest Railway Station: Newport
Nearest Bus Station: Newport
Club Shop: At the ground
Opening Times: Matchdays only
Telephone Nº: (01633) 662262
Police Telephone Nº: (01633) 244999

GROUND INFORMATION

Away Supporters' Entrances & Sections:
No segregation unless specifically required by Police

ADMISSION INFO (2009/2010 PRICES)

Adult Standing: £10.00
Adult Seating: £10.00
Senior Citizen Standing: £7.00
Senior Citizen Seating: £7.00
Full-time Student Seating/Standing: £6.00
Under-16s Seating/Standing: £3.00
Programme Price: £2.50

DISABLED INFORMATION

Wheelchairs: Accommodated
Helpers: Admitted
Prices: Normal prices for the disabled. Free for helpers
Disabled Toilets: Yes
Contact: (01633) 662262 (Bookings are not necessary)

Travelling Supporters' Information:
Routes: Exit the M4 at Junction 24 and take the A48 exit at the roundabout, signposted 'Newport Int. Sports Village'. Go straight on at the first two roundabouts then bear left at the 3rd roundabout. Carry straight on over the next two roundabouts, then turn left before the Carcraft site. Take the 1st turning on the left into the Stadium car park.

ST. ALBANS CITY FC

Founded: 1908
Former Names: None
Nickname: 'The Saints'
Ground: Clarence Park, York Road, St. Albans, Hertfordshire AL1 4PL
Record Attendance: 9,757 (27th February 1926)
Pitch Size: 110 × 80 yards

Colours: Blue shirts with Yellow trim, Yellow shorts
Telephone No: (01727) 864296
Fax Number: (01727) 866235
Ground Capacity: 5,007
Seating Capacity: 667
Web site: www.sacfc.co.uk

GENERAL INFORMATION

Supporters Club: Ian Rogers, c/o Club
Telephone No: –
Car Parking: Street parking
Coach Parking: In Clarence Park
Nearest Railway Station: St. Albans City (200 yds)
Club Shop: At the ground
Opening Times: Matchdays only
Telephone No: (01727) 864296
Police Telephone No: (01727) 276122

GROUND INFORMATION

Away Supporters' Entrances & Sections:
Hatfield Road End when matches are segregated

ADMISSION INFO (2009/2010 PRICES)

Adult Standing: £10.00
Adult Seating: £12.00
Under-12s Standing: £3.00   **OAP/Under-16s**: £5.00
Under-12s Seating: £4.00   **OAP/Under-16s**: £6.00
Programme Price: £2.50

DISABLED INFORMATION

Wheelchairs: Accommodated
Helpers: One admitted per disabled supporter
Prices: Free for the disabled, concessionary prices for the helpers
Disabled Toilets: Available inside the building at the York Road End
Contact: (01727) 864296   (Bookings are not necessary)

Travelling Supporters' Information:
Routes: Take the M1 or M10 to the A405 North Orbital Road and at the roundabout at the start of the M10, go north on the A5183 (Watling Street). Turn right along St. Stephen's Hill and carry along into St. Albans. Continue up Holywell Hill, go through two sets of traffic lights and at the end of St. Peter's Street, take a right turn at the roundabout into Hatfield Road. Follow over the mini-roundabouts and at the second set of traffic lights turn left into Clarence Road and the ground is on the left. Park in Clarence Road and enter the ground via the Park or in York Road and use the entrance by the footbridge.

STAINES TOWN FC

Founded: 1892
Former Names: Staines FC, Staines Vale FC, Staines Albany FC, Staines Projectile FC & Staines Lagonda FC
Nickname: 'The Swans'
Ground: Wheatsheaf Park, Wheatsheaf Lane, Staines   TW18 2PD
Record Attendance: 2,860 (2007)
Pitch Size: 110 × 76 yards

Ground Capacity: 3,000
Seating Capacity: 432
Colours: Old Gold and Blue shirts with Blue shorts
Telephone Nº: (01784) 225943
Office Number: (01784) 225943
Correspondence Address: Steve Parsons, 3 Birch Green, Staines   TW18 4HA
Web site: www.stainesmassive.co.uk

GENERAL INFORMATION
Supporters Club: None
Car Parking: Large car park shared with The Thames Club
Coach Parking: At the ground
Nearest Railway Station: Staines (1 mile)
Nearest Bus Station: Staines Central (1 mile)
Club Shop: At the ground
Opening Times: Matchdays only
Telephone Nº: (01784) 225943

GROUND INFORMATION
Away Supporters' Entrances & Sections:
No usual segregation

ADMISSION INFO (2009/2010 PRICES)
Adult Standing: £10.00
Adult Seating: £10.00
Senior Citizen/Junior Standing: £5.00
Senior Citizen/Junior Seating: £5.00
Programme Price: £2.00

DISABLED INFORMATION
Wheelchairs: Accommodated
Helpers: Admitted
Prices: Concessionary prices apply for the disabled
Disabled Toilets: Available
Contact: (01784) 225943

Travelling Supporters' Information:
Routes: Exit the M25 at Junction 13 and take the A30 towards London. At the 'Crooked Billet' roundabout follow signs for Staines Town Centre. Pass under the bridge and bear left, passing the Elmsleigh Centre Car Parks and bear left at the next junction (opposite the Thames Lodge Hotel) into Laleham Road. Pass under the iron railway bridge by the river and continue along for ¾ mile. Turn right by the bollards into Wheatsheaf Lane and the ground is situated on the left by the Thames Club.

THURROCK FC

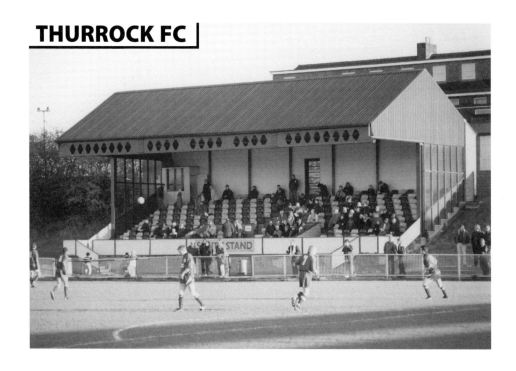

Founded: 1985
Former Names: Purfleet FC
Nickname: 'Fleet'
Ground: Thurrock Hotel, Ship Lane, Grays, Essex, RM19 1YN **Telephone Nº:** (01708) 865492
Record Attendance: 2,572 (1998)
Pitch Size: 113 × 72 yards

Colours: Yellow and Green shirts with Green shorts
Tel Nº: (01708) 865492 (Clubhouse)
Contact Nº: (01708) 458301 (Secretary)
Fax Number: (01708) 868863
Ground Capacity: 4,200
Seating Capacity: 500
Web site: www.thurrock-fc.com

GENERAL INFORMATION
Supporters Club: None
Car Parking: At the ground
Coach Parking: At the ground
Nearest Railway Station: Purfleet (2 miles)
Nearest Bus Station: Grays Town Centre
Club Shop: At the ground
Opening Times: Matchdays only
Telephone Nº: (01708) 865492
Police Telephone Nº: (01375) 391212

GROUND INFORMATION
Away Supporters' Entrances & Sections:
No usual segregation

ADMISSION INFO (2009/2010 PRICES)
Adult Standing: £10.00
Adult Seating: £10.00
Child Standing: £2.00
Child Seating: £2.00
Senior Citizen Standing: £6.00
Senior Citizen Seating: £6.00
Programme Price: £2.00

DISABLED INFORMATION
Wheelchairs: No special area but accommodated
Helpers: Admitted
Prices: Free for the disabled. Helpers pay normal prices
Disabled Toilets: Available in the Clubhouse
Contact: (01708) 865492 (Bookings are not necessary)

Travelling Supporters' Information:
Routes: Take the M25 or A13 to the Dartford Tunnel roundabout. The ground is then 50 yards on the right along Ship Lane.

WELLING UNITED FC

Founded: 1963
Former Names: None
Nickname: 'The Wings'
Ground: Park View Road Ground, Welling, Kent, DA16 1SY
Record Attendance: 4,020 (1989/90)
Pitch Size: 112 × 72 yards

Colours: Shirts are Red with White facings, Red shorts
Telephone Nº: (0208) 301-1196
Daytime Phone Nº: (0208) 301-1196
Fax Number: (0208) 301-5676
Ground Capacity: 4,000
Seating Capacity: 500
Web site: www.wellingunited.com

GENERAL INFORMATION
Supporters Club: –
Car Parking: Street parking only
Coach Parking: Outside of the ground
Nearest Railway Station: Welling (¾ mile)
Nearest Bus Station: Bexleyheath
Club Shop: At the ground
Opening Times: Matchdays only
Telephone Nº: (0208) 301-1196
Police Telephone Nº: (0208) 304-3161

GROUND INFORMATION
Away Supporters' Entrances & Sections:
Accommodation in the Danson Park End

ADMISSION INFO (2009/2010 PRICES)
Adult Standing: £10.00
Adult Seating: £11.00
Senior Citizen/Child Standing: £6.00
Senior Citizen/Child Seating: £7.00
Under-12s: £3.00
Programme Price: £2.00

DISABLED INFORMATION
Wheelchairs: Accommodated at the side of the Main Stand
Helpers: Admitted
Prices: £6.00 for the disabled. Helpers pay normal prices
Disabled Toilets: Yes
Contact: (0208) 301-1196   (Bookings are not necessary)

Travelling Supporters' Information:
Routes: Take the A2 (Rochester Way) from London, then the A221 Northwards (Danson Road) to Bexleyheath. At the end turn left towards Welling along Park View Road and the ground is on the left.

WESTON-SUPER-MARE FC

Founded: 1899
Former Names: Christ Church Old Boys FC
Nickname: 'Seagulls'
Ground: Woodspring Stadium, Winterstoke Road,
Weston-Super-Mare   BS24 9AA
Record Attendance: 2,623 (vs Woking in F.A. Cup)
Pitch Size: 110 × 70 yards

Colours: White shirts with Black shorts
Telephone Nº: (01934) 621618
Fax Number: (01934) 622704
Ground Capacity: 3,071
Seating Capacity: 320
Web site: www.westonsupermareafc.co.uk

GENERAL INFORMATION

Supporters Club: Joe Varian, 336 Milton Road, Weston-Super-Mare
Telephone Nº: (01934) 627929
Car Parking: 140 spaces available at the ground
Coach Parking: At the ground
Nearest Railway Station: Weston-Super-Mare (1½ miles)
Nearest Bus Station: Weston-Super-Mare (1½ miles)
Club Shop: At the ground
Opening Times: Matchdays only
Telephone Nº: (01934) 621618
Police Telephone Nº: (01275) 818181

GROUND INFORMATION

Away Supporters' Entrances & Sections:
No usual segregation

ADMISSION INFO (2009/2010 PRICES)

Adult Standing/Seating: £10.00
Senior Citizen/Student Standing/Seating: £6.50
Under-16s Standing/Seating: Free of charge (proof of age required) – £2.00 without ID
Programme Price: £2.00

DISABLED INFORMATION

Wheelchairs: Accommodated in a special disabled section
Helpers: Admitted
Prices: Normal prices apply
Disabled Toilets: Two available
Contact: (01934) 621618   (Bookings are not necessary)

Travelling Supporters' Information:
Routes: Exit the M5 at Junction 21 and follow the dual carriageway (A370) to the 4th roundabout (Asda Winterstoke). Turn left, go over the mini-roundabout and continue for 800 yards. The ground is on the right.

WEYMOUTH FC

Founded: 1890
Former Names: None
Nickname: 'Terras'
Ground: Wessex Stadium, Radipole Lane, Weymouth, Dorset DT4 9XJ
Record Attendance: 6,500 (14th November 2005)
Pitch Size: 115 × 74 yards

Colours: Shirts are Claret and Sky Blue, Claret shorts
Telephone Nº: (01305) 785558
Fax Number: (01305) 766658
Ground Capacity: 6,500
Seating Capacity: 800
Web site: www.theterras.co.uk

GENERAL INFORMATION
Supporters Club: Nigel Beckett, c/o Club
Telephone Nº: (01305) 785558
Car Parking: 200 spaces available at the ground
Coach Parking: At the ground
Nearest Railway Station: Weymouth (2 miles)
Nearest Bus Station: Weymouth Town Centre
Club Shop: At the ground
Opening Times: Matchdays only
Telephone Nº: –
Police Telephone Nº: (01305) 251212

GROUND INFORMATION
Away Supporters' Entrances & Sections:
Visitors End turnstiles and accommodation when segregation is used

ADMISSION INFO (2009/2010 PRICES)
Adult Standing: £11.00
Adult Seating: £13.00 (£19.00 in the Premier Stand)
Senior Citizen/Student Standing: £9.00
Senior Citizen/Student Seating: £7.00 (£13 in Premier)
Under-16s Standing: £4.00
Under-16s Seating: £6.00 (£9.00 in the Premier Stand)
Note: Family tickets are also available at discounted rates when purchased in advance
Programme Price: £2.00

DISABLED INFORMATION
Wheelchairs: Accommodated
Helpers: Admitted
Prices: Normal prices apply for the disabled. Free for helpers
Disabled Toilets: Yes
Contact: (01305) 785558   (Bookings are not necessary)

Travelling Supporters' Information:
Routes: Take the A354 from Dorchester to Weymouth and turn right at the first roundabout to the town centre. Take the 3rd exit at the next roundabout and follow signs for the ground which is about ½ mile on the right.

WOKING FC

Founded: 1889
Former Names: None
Nickname: 'Cardinals'
Ground: Kingfield Stadium, Kingfield, Woking, Surrey GU22 9AA
Record Attendance: 6,000 (1997)
Pitch Size: 109 × 76 yards

Colours: Shirts are Red & White halves, Black shorts
Telephone Nº: (01483) 772470
Daytime Phone Nº: (01483) 772470
Fax Number: (01483) 888423
Ground Capacity: 6,161
Seating Capacity: 2,511
Web site: www.wokingfc.co.uk

GENERAL INFORMATION

Supporters Club: Mr. G. Burnett (Secretary), c/o Club
Telephone Nº: (01483) 772470
Car Parking: Limited parking at the ground
Coach Parking: At or opposite the ground
Nearest Railway Station: Woking (1 mile)
Nearest Bus Station: Woking
Club Shop: At the ground
Opening Times: Weekdays and Matchdays
Telephone Nº: (01483) 772470
Police Telephone Nº: (01483) 761991

GROUND INFORMATION

Away Supporters' Entrances & Sections:
Kingfield Road when segregation is in force

ADMISSION INFO (2009/2010 PRICES)

Adult Standing: £12.00
Adult Seating: £12.00
Under-16s/Student Standing: £2.00
Under-16s/Student Seating: £2.00
Senior Citizen Standing: £8.00
Senior Citizen Seating: £8.00
Programme Price: £2.50

DISABLED INFORMATION

Wheelchairs: 8 spaces in the Leslie Gosden Stand and 8 spaces in front of the Family Stand
Helpers: Admitted
Prices: One wheelchair and helper for £11.00
Disabled Toilets: Yes – in the Leslie Gosden Stand and Family Stand area
Contact: (01483) 772470 (Bookings are necessary)

Travelling Supporters' Information:
Routes: Exit the M25 at Junction 10 and follow the A3 towards Guildford. Leave at the next junction onto the B2215 through Ripley and join the A247 to Woking. Alternatively, exit the M25 at Junction 11 and follow the A320 to Woking Town Centre. The ground is on the outskirts of Woking – follow signs on the A320 and A247.

WORCESTER CITY FC

Founded: 1902
Former Names: Berwick Rangers FC
Nickname: 'The City'
Ground: St.Georges Lane, Worcester   WR1 1QT
Record Attendance: 17,042 (1958/59)
Pitch Size: 110 × 75 yards

Colours: Blue and White shirts, Royal Blue shorts
Telephone Nº: (01905) 23003
Fax Number: (01905) 26668
Ground Capacity: 4,500
Seating Capacity: 1,100
Web site: www.worcestercityfc.co.uk

GENERAL INFORMATION

Supporters Club: P.Gardner, c/o Club
Telephone Nº: –
Car Parking: Street parking
Coach Parking: Street parking
Nearest Railway Station: Foregate Street (1 mile)
Nearest Bus Station: Crowngate Bus Station
Club Shop: At the ground
Opening Times: Monday to Friday and Matchdays from
10.00am to 5.00pm
Telephone Nº: (01905) 23003
Police Telephone Nº: (01905) 723888

GROUND INFORMATION

Away Supporters' Entrances & Sections:
Turnstile at the Canal End when segregation in in force for
Canal End accommodation

ADMISSION INFO (2009/2010 PRICES)

Adult Standing: £11.00
Adult Seating: £12.00
Under-16s Standing: £3.00
Under-16s Seating: £4.00
Note: One child (Under-16) is admitted free of charge when
accompanied by a paying adult.
Senior Citizen Standing: £5.00
Senior Citizen Seating: £6.00
Programme Price: £2.00

DISABLED INFORMATION

Wheelchairs: 3 covered spaces available
Helpers: Please phone the club for information
Prices: Please phone the club for information
Disabled Toilets: None
Contact: (01905) 23003   (Bookings are necessary)

Travelling Supporters' Information:
Routes: Exit the M5 at Junction 6 and take the A449 Kidderminster Road. Follow to the end of the dual carriageway and take
the second exit at the roundabout for Worcester City Centre. At the first set of traffic lights turn right into the town centre. The
3rd turning on the left is St.Georges Lane.

Blue Square Premier — 2008/2009 Season

	Altrincham	Barrow	Burton Albion	Cambridge United	Crawley Town	Eastbourne Borough	Ebbsfleet United	Forest Green Rovers	Grays Athletic	Histon	Kettering Town	Kidderminster Harriers	Lewes	Mansfield Town	Northwich Victoria	Oxford United	Rushden & Diamonds	Salisbury City	Stevenage Borough	Torquay United	Weymouth	Woking	Wrexham	York City
Altrincham	■	3-4	1-3	1-0	2-2	2-2	2-0	2-5	2-0	0-1	1-1	2-2	1-0	1-0	1-0	1-0	0-4	0-0	1-2	0-1	4-0	1-0	1-1	1-1
Barrow	2-2	■	0-0	0-2	3-3	3-1	0-3	3-1	1-1	1-0	2-4	1-0	2-0	2-1	0-0	3-0	1-1	0-0	1-3	1-1	0-1	0-1	1-1	0-0
Burton Albion	1-1	2-1	■	3-1	2-1	2-0	3-1	4-2	4-0	3-1	1-1	2-2	5-2	1-0	1-1	0-1	3-0	1-2	2-0	0-1	1-1	3-2	2-1	2-1
Cambridge United	0-0	2-1	2-0	■	1-1	2-1	1-0	0-1	1-0	2-2	0-2	2-1	1-0	2-1	4-1	1-1	0-0	4-0	1-1	0-1	1-0	4-1	2-0	1-0
Crawley Town	4-0	4-0	4-0	2-2	■	1-0	1-2	2-2	2-1	3-3	1-0	2-0	5-1	2-1	5-2	0-1	0-0	0-3	0-2	3-1	4-2	2-2	1-0	0-1
Eastbourne Borough	1-0	0-2	1-2	0-3	2-1	■	0-1	1-0	2-1	1-1	1-2	2-3	1-0	1-2	4-1	0-3	0-1	0-0	2-1	4-2	3-0	0-0	1-0	2-1
Ebbsfleet United	1-0	1-0	2-1	1-1	4-4	1-1	■	0-1	0-1	0-1	0-0	1-1	2-1	2-2	1-0	1-1	1-0	2-2	4-0	0-2	1-0	2-0	1-0	0-0
Forest Green Rovers	1-3	2-1	2-3	2-2	1-0	1-2	1-4	■	1-1	2-2	0-2	2-2	4-1	1-0	3-0	3-3	4-0	1-2	0-3	1-2	4-1	0-2	2-3	1-1
Grays Athletic	2-1	2-1	0-1	0-1	1-0	0-1	3-1	2-1	■	1-4	1-1	3-2	0-0	2-1	2-1	2-0	0-0	3-1	1-2	1-2	1-1	1-1	2-1	1-0
Histon	1-0	2-0	4-3	1-1	1-0	3-3	5-2	0-1	4-1	■	1-0	1-1	1-1	3-0	2-1	5-2	0-0	2-0	0-0	1-1	1-0	1-0	1-0	1-1
Kettering Town	3-1	0-0	0-1	1-2	1-1	0-1	2-1	1-1	0-0	1-0	■	1-0	1-0	1-3	2-1	1-2	1-1	1-0	1-0	2-1	0-1	1-0	1-0	4-2
Kidderminster Harriers	4-0	0-1	2-1	1-3	2-0	2-0	3-1	1-1	2-0	2-0	0-1	■	1-1	2-0	1-2	1-0	2-1	3-2	4-2	1-0	0-2	3-0	1-0	2-0
Lewes	2-0	0-3	0-1	0-2	0-3	0-2	0-0	3-2	2-0	0-3	1-2	0-1	■	0-1	2-3	2-1	0-4	1-4	0-2	0-2	1-0	0-2	0-2	1-1
Mansfield Town	2-0	2-2	0-2	1-1	1-0	3-1	2-0	3-0	1-0	1-0	0-0	4-2	1-0	■	3-2	1-3	0-0	3-0	2-1	1-1	2-1	0-1	1-2	1-0
Northwich Victoria	0-1	2-1	0-1	0-1	0-1	1-2	2-0	0-0	2-0	1-2	0-0	1-1	3-0	2-0	■	1-2	4-2	1-1	0-1	2-3	2-3	2-0	1-2	2-2
Oxford United	1-0	3-0	2-1	3-1	1-2	6-3	5-1	2-1	4-1	2-1	1-1	1-0	2-1	1-0	1-2	■	2-1	2-0	1-1	0-2	1-0	0-0	1-0	1-0
Rushden & Diamonds	1-1	1-1	2-1	1-2	0-1	2-0	2-0	2-2	1-1	1-2	1-0	1-0	2-1	0-1	2-1	1-0	■	2-1	1-1	1-3	1-0	3-1	1-1	2-0
Salisbury City	1-3	3-0	0-1	1-2	2-0	2-0	1-0	2-2	1-0	0-4	1-2	0-0	1-2	2-3	1-1	2-1	1-1	■	2-4	2-2	1-0	1-0	1-4	1-1
Stevenage Borough	3-0	3-0	4-1	2-1	1-1	1-3	1-1	1-1	0-0	1-3	2-1	3-1	3-0	3-2	1-1	1-1	3-1	2-0	■	0-0	1-1	1-0	1-2	3-3
Torquay United	3-1	4-1	2-1	0-0	0-2	2-0	0-2	3-3	1-1	4-1	2-0	4-1	2-1	1-1	1-1	0-1	3-0	2-1	3-0	■	0-2	2-1	1-1	1-1
Weymouth	2-0	0-3	0-5	2-2	2-2	3-2	0-2	1-1	3-1	2-5	0-2	1-2	2-0	1-1	3-0	2-2	0-9	0-4	0-3	0-1	■	1-1	1-3	1-2
Woking	1-2	1-0	0-0	0-1	0-0	0-4	1-0	0-1	3-1	1-0	0-1	1-5	1-1	2-2	4-1	0-2	1-1	1-0	0-1	2-2	1-1	■	1-1	0-2
Wrexham	0-1	1-1	0-1	2-0	0-2	5-0	3-2	1-1	3-2	0-0	2-1	0-1	2-0	2-0	3-3	2-0	0-3	1-1	5-0	1-1	2-0	1-1	■	3-1
York City	1-2	1-1	1-3	0-0	2-2	1-0	3-1	2-1	0-1	1-1	0-0	0-0	3-0	1-1	1-2	0-0	2-0	1-1	0-2	1-2	2-0	2-0	1-0	■

Blue Square Premier (Football Conference)

Season 2008/2009

Burton Albion	46	27	7	12	81	52	88
Cambridge United	46	24	14	8	65	39	86
Histon	46	23	14	9	78	48	83
Torquay United	46	23	14	9	72	47	83
Stevenage Borough	46	23	12	11	73	54	81
Kidderminster Harriers	46	23	10	13	69	48	79
Oxford United	46	24	10	12	72	51	77
Kettering Town	46	21	13	12	50	37	76
Crawley Town	46	19	14	13	77	55	70
Wrexham	46	18	12	16	64	48	66
Rushden & Diamonds	46	16	15	15	61	50	63
Mansfield Town	46	19	9	18	57	55	62
Eastbourne Borough	46	18	6	22	58	70	60
Ebbsfleet United	46	16	10	20	52	60	58
Altrincham	46	15	11	20	49	66	56
Salisbury City	46	14	13	19	54	64	55
York City	46	11	19	16	47	51	52
Forest Green Rovers	46	12	16	18	70	76	52
Grays Athletic	46	14	10	22	44	64	52
Barrow	46	12	15	19	51	65	51
Woking	46	10	14	22	37	60	44
Northwich Victoria	46	11	10	25	56	75	43
Weymouth	46	11	10	25	45	86	43
Lewes	46	6	6	34	28	89	24

Oxford United had 5 points deducted.
Mansfield Town had 4 points deducted.
Crawley Town had 1 point deducted.

Promotion Play-offs

Stevenage Borough 3   Cambridge United 1
Torquay United 2   Histon 0

Cambridge United 3   Stevenage Borough ..... 0 (aet)
Cambridge United won 4-3 on aggregate.

Histon 1   Torquay United 0
Torquay United won 2-1 on aggregate

Cambridge United 0   Torquay United 2

Promoted: Burton Albion and Torquay United
Relegated: Woking, Northwich Victoria, Weymouth and Lewes

Blue Square North 2008/2009 Season

	AFC Telford United	Alfreton Town	Blyth Spartans	Burscough	Droylsden	Farsley Celtic	Fleetwood Town	Gainsborough Trinity	Gateshead	Harrogate Town	Hinckley United	Hucknall Town	Hyde United	King's Lynn	Redditch United	Solihull Moors	Southport	Stafford Rangers	Stalybridge Celtic	Tamworth	Vauxhall Motors	Workington
AFC Telford United	■	0-0	2-1	3-0	2-0	2-0	0-0	2-1	1-0	3-1	4-2	3-1	2-3	1-1	1-1	3-0	1-0	0-1	1-0	0-0	5-1	0-0
Alfreton Town	3-1	■	1-1	2-0	2-3	3-1	3-3	1-4	1-3	4-1	1-1	5-0	3-2	1-1	2-0	4-1	2-0	2-0	2-1	1-1	3-1	0-0
Blyth Spartans	2-0	2-2	■	0-2	0-2	5-0	3-0	1-1	0-1	3-4	1-0	3-0	3-0	2-4	1-0	3-0	1-0	2-1	0-0	0-4	0-1	3-1
Burscough	0-2	1-3	2-3	■	0-1	0-0	1-1	0-2	2-4	0-2	1-1	2-3	2-2	1-1	1-0	1-2	2-3	2-0	0-2	0-1	0-1	2-1
Droylsden	1-0	2-0	2-0	3-1	■	2-0	1-3	3-2	0-0	2-1	3-0	5-1	2-1	1-0	2-2	2-1	0-0	0-1	1-1	1-1	1-2	1-1
Farsley Celtic	1-0	3-3	3-0	5-1	1-1	■	4-1	2-1	0-1	1-0	2-3	4-0	2-1	1-1	1-2	0-1	5-1	4-0	2-3	1-3	0-1	0-5
Fleetwood Town	1-0	1-1	1-0	3-1	2-1	2-1	■	2-2	0-2	1-0	1-0	1-3	1-3	3-0	3-1	2-1	1-1	2-2	1-2	1-2	2-0	1-0
Gainsborough Trinity	1-2	0-2	0-0	0-4	1-0	0-0	3-4	■	0-0	3-2	3-1	2-2	0-1	2-0	4-1	1-1	0-1	0-3	3-3	0-1	1-1	1-2
Gateshead	1-1	3-0	3-0	4-1	1-1	3-0	2-2	1-0	■	1-3	5-0	1-0	6-3	3-2	2-0	3-0	1-0	0-1	1-0	5-1	2-2	2-1
Harrogate Town	2-0	2-2	3-1	2-0	1-1	1-0	5-2	0-3	1-0	■	2-2	2-0	2-1	4-0	1-1	4-0	0-3	3-3	0-1	2-2	2-0	0-1
Hinckley United	0-2	1-1	2-1	0-1	1-0	1-2	2-1	0-2	2-0	2-0	■	4-0	0-1	1-0	4-2	0-0	1-1	4-0	0-1	1-3	2-3	1-0
Hucknall Town	0-5	1-1	1-1	0-2	1-1	1-2	3-2	1-2	2-2	1-1	1-2	■	0-1	1-2	0-2	0-2	0-0	3-1	2-3	2-3	0-1	0-0
Hyde United	0-4	1-1	1-0	0-1	1-3	3-1	5-3	0-0	2-5	2-3	0-0	2-0	■	0-1	1-2	3-1	1-1	1-1	0-2	1-2	3-1	4-4
King's Lynn	1-1	0-4	2-3	0-0	2-2	1-4	1-0	2-2	2-0	2-3	1-1	0-0	4-1	■	1-1	3-0	0-0	2-2	1-0	1-2	1-1	1-3
Redditch United	0-1	2-2	2-0	1-2	0-4	3-1	1-1	1-1	0-2	2-1	0-2	2-2	1-0	1-2	■	0-0	0-2	2-2	0-1	1-1	2-1	2-0
Solihull Moors	1-3	2-2	2-0	3-2	2-1	2-1	2-3	2-0	1-1	1-3	3-1	2-2	1-1	2-1		■	0-2	0-1	0-1	1-1	3-2	2-0
Southport	1-1	0-1	2-1	3-0	3-1	1-0	1-1	5-3	2-3	1-0	0-0	3-0	2-0	2-1	2-3	3-0	■	3-2	2-0	0-1	5-2	0-0
Stafford Rangers	1-3	0-2	1-0	0-2	0-0	1-0	1-2	2-0	4-1	0-0	3-1	0-0	2-0	0-0	0-1	0-2	0-3	■	0-1	0-1	0-1	0-0
Stalybridge Celtic	2-2	0-2	2-0	4-0	2-2	1-0	0-5	1-2	1-2	1-3	7-1	2-2	4-1	1-1	3-3	5-0	0-1	2-0	■	2-2	1-0	1-4
Tamworth	0-1	1-2	1-1	6-2	2-0	2-1	2-1	0-0	2-1	3-1	1-0	1-1	2-0	2-0	1-1	1-0	1-1	1-2	0-3	■	2-0	1-0
Vauxhall Motors	2-0	1-1	2-1	2-0	1-4	2-0	0-2	1-1	1-2	1-0	0-4	2-3	2-1	1-3	1-1	2-2	0-0	1-1	1-1	2-2	■	3-0
Workington	1-0	0-3	0-1	4-1	1-1	0-2	3-2	5-0	4-2	0-0	1-3	1-0	2-2	1-1	0-1	2-1	0-1	2-2	0-2	1-4	3-1	■

Blue Square North (Football Conference)

Season 2008/2009

Tamworth	42	24	13	5	70	41	85
Gateshead	42	24	8	10	81	48	80
Alfreton Town	42	20	17	5	81	48	77
AFC Telford United	42	22	10	10	65	34	76
Southport	42	21	13	8	63	36	76
Stalybridge Celtic	42	20	10	12	71	50	70
Droylsden	42	18	14	10	64	44	68
Fleetwood Town	42	17	11	14	70	66	62
Harrogate Town	42	17	10	15	66	57	61
Hinckley United	42	16	9	17	56	59	57
Vauxhall Motors	42	14	11	17	51	67	53
Workington	42	13	12	17	54	55	51
Gainsborough Trinity	42	12	14	16	57	63	50
Redditch United	42	12	14	16	49	61	50
Blyth Spartans	42	14	7	21	50	58	49
Solihull Moors	42	13	10	19	49	73	49
Kings Lynn	42	10	18	14	50	60	48
Stafford Rangers	42	12	12	18	41	56	48
Farsley Celtic	42	14	5	23	58	65	47
Hyde United	42	11	9	22	57	80	42
Burscough	42	10	6	26	43	80	36
Hucknall Town	42	5	13	24	39	84	28

Promotion Play-offs North

Southport .... 0 Gateshead 1
AFC Telford United .... 2 Alfreton Town 0

Gateshead .... 1 Southport 1
Gateshead won 2-1 on aggregate

Alfreton Town .... 4 AFC Telford United 3
AFC Telford United won 5-4 on aggregate

Gateshead .... 1 AFC Telford United 0

Promoted: Tamworth and Gateshead

Blue Square South
2008/2009 Season

	AFC Wimbledon	Basingstoke Town	Bath City	Bishop's Stortford	Bognor Regis Town	Braintree Town	Bromley	Chelmsford City	Dorchester Town	Eastleigh	Fisher Athltic	Hampton & Richmond Borough	Havant & Waterlooville	Hayes & Yeading United	Maidenhead United	Newport County	St. Albans City	Team Bath	Thurrock	Welling United	Weston Super Mare	Worcester City
AFC Wimbledon		1-0	3-2	4-1	3-1	5-1	3-1	3-1	2-0	0-2	3-0	1-1	3-0	2-0	3-1	3-0	3-0	2-0	2-1	0-1	1-1	2-0
Basingstoke Town	0-1		1-0	1-1	0-0	2-2	2-0	1-2	0-0	1-0	2-2	1-1	2-2	1-1	0-1	0-0	1-2	1-3	1-0	0-0	0-1	0-0
Bath City	2-2	1-0		2-3	0-1	3-2	1-3	2-1	2-0	1-1	1-0	0-1	2-1	0-1	1-0	2-1	1-0	1-1	2-2	0-4	3-0	1-0
Bishop's Stortford	0-1	3-2	0-2		2-0	0-3	1-1	2-1	0-2	3-4	0-1	1-3	1-0	0-0	2-0	1-1	1-1	4-3	2-1	0-1	2-1	3-0
Bognor Regis Town	1-5	2-3	0-2	0-2		0-2	1-1	2-1	0-0	1-0	2-1	0-1	1-5	1-1	2-4	0-1	0-5	3-0	1-1	0-0	1-1	1-2
Braintree Town	0-1	0-1	0-4	2-0	1-1		2-0	1-2	0-1	1-1	2-0	1-2	1-0	0-1	0-2	3-2	1-0	4-1	1-2	1-1	1-1	1-1
Bromley	2-2	0-2	1-1	1-0	1-0	1-4		2-2	1-0	5-1	3-0	0-2	2-2	1-0	1-2	2-1	2-3	4-0	3-3	1-3	3-0	0-2
Chelmsford City	3-2	2-2	2-3	3-3	2-0	1-1	0-1		2-1	3-0	3-0	3-2	1-2	2-1	2-1	0-0	1-1	1-1	3-2	2-0	4-1	2-0
Dorchester Town	1-1	0-0	0-2	0-2	1-0	2-2	2-1	0-1		0-4	3-0	0-1	1-0	1-2	0-3	0-1	1-1	2-2	4-3	1-1	1-2	3-1
Eastleigh	2-1	1-0	2-0	1-1	2-1	2-1	1-0	2-1	0-1		3-0	2-1	2-0	3-3	0-0	3-2	3-0	1-3	1-1	4-2	1-0	1-0
Fisher Athletic	0-3	1-0	1-0	0-3	0-1	0-2	0-2	0-1	4-0	1-2		0-2	1-1	0-5	0-1	1-3	0-4	0-6	0-3	0-5	0-2	0-1
Hampton & Richmond Borough	1-1	0-0	3-1	2-1	0-0	2-1	1-1	4-1	2-0	3-0	3-0		2-1	2-3	1-0	0-1	0-0	3-0	3-1	2-0	4-1	1-2
Havant & Waterlooville	0-0	5-1	0-0	3-0	2-2	1-1	0-1	1-1	1-2	2-2	3-0	1-4		2-2	3-3	1-1	2-0	2-1	2-2	1-0	2-3	0-2
Hayes & Yeading United	2-1	5-0	2-2	1-0	3-1	0-1	2-1	0-1	2-1	0-1	3-4	0-0	2-1		2-0	2-0	2-1	1-1	2-1	2-1	3-0	3-1
Maidenhead United	0-4	1-2	0-0	3-2	2-0	2-1	4-0	0-2	2-1	1-4	1-0	0-3	1-0	2-0		0-1	1-0	0-2	1-1	2-0	0-0	5-0
Newport County	1-4	3-0	0-4	0-1	2-1	2-1	3-0	3-1	4-4	0-1	4-0	1-0	0-2	1-5	0-1		0-1	4-2	1-1	0-0	1-0	1-0
St. Albans City	0-0	3-0	2-1	2-0	1-0	0-3	4-5	1-2	2-0	5-0	4-1	2-2	1-1	1-1	1-2	1-1		0-0	0-2	2-3	3-0	0-2
Team Bath	1-2	1-2	0-1	2-2	1-0	0-3	0-3	2-0	4-1	1-3	4-2	1-0	4-1	0-2	2-0	2-0	2-0		4-1	0-1	1-2	0-2
Thurrock	0-1	6-0	2-0	1-3	1-1	1-0	1-1	0-1	1-0	0-1	2-1	3-3	2-3	0-1	1-2	0-0	0-0	1-2		1-2	0-1	2-0
Welling United	2-2	1-1	2-1	1-3	4-1	1-0	3-1	1-3	0-0	3-2	3-0	4-0	2-1	0-2	1-1	0-2	0-1	1-1	0-0		2-0	1-3
Weston Super Mare	1-1	0-3	0-1	2-1	1-2	3-1	2-1	1-4	2-2	1-1	3-1	0-3	0-1	1-2	2-2	1-1	1-1	0-1	2-1	0-3		1-1
Worcester City	3-2	0-0	0-1	1-3	1-1	2-2	1-0	0-1	0-0	0-1	1-1	1-2	2-2	0-3	1-1	0-0	2-0	0-2	0-2	2-0	1-2	

Blue Square South (Football Conference)
Season 2008/2009

AFC Wimbledon	42	26	10	6	86	36	88
Hampton & Richmond Borough	42	25	10	7	74	37	85
Eastleigh	42	25	8	9	69	49	83
Hayes & Yeading United	42	24	9	9	74	43	81
Chelmsford City	42	23	8	11	72	52	77
Maidenhead United	42	21	8	13	57	46	71
Welling United	42	19	11	12	61	44	68
Bath City	42	20	8	14	56	45	68
Bishop's Stortford	42	17	8	17	60	60	59
Newport County	42	16	11	15	50	51	59
Team Bath	42	16	7	19	62	64	55
St. Albans City	42	14	12	16	56	50	54
Bromley	42	15	9	18	60	64	54
Braintree Town	42	14	10	18	57	54	52
Havant & Waterlooville	42	11	15	16	59	58	48
Worcester City	42	12	11	19	38	53	47
Weston Super Mare	42	12	11	19	43	68	47
Basingstoke Town	42	10	16	16	36	55	46
Dorchester Town	42	10	12	20	39	61	42
Thurrock	42	9	13	20	54	60	40
Bognor Regis Town	42	7	12	23	33	68	26
Fisher Athletic	42	5	3	34	22	100	18

Bognor Regis Town had 7 points deducted

Promotion Play-offs South

Chelmsford City 1   Hampton & Richmond Bor. 3
Hayes & Yeading United 2   Eastleigh 4

Hampton & Richmond Bor. 0   Chelmsford City 0
Hampton & Richmond Borough won 3-1 on aggregate
Eastleigh 0   Hayes & Yeading United 4
Hayes & Yeading United won 6-2 on aggregate

Hampton & Richmond Bor. 2   Hayes & Yeading United 3

Promoted: AFC Wimbledon and Hayes & Yeading United

Northern Premier League Premier Division 2008/2009 Season	Ashton United	Boston United	Bradford Park Avenue	Buxton	Cammell Laird	Eastwood Town	FC United of Manchester	Frickley Athletic	Guiseley	Hednesford Town	Ilkeston Town	Kendal Town	Leigh Genesis	Marine	Matlock Town	Nantwich Town	North Ferriby United	Ossett Town	Prescot Cables	Whitby Town	Witton Albion	Worksop Town
Ashton United		3-0	2-1	4-1	1-1	2-2	2-1	0-2	2-2	1-0	1-1	1-2	2-0	2-0	3-2	0-1	1-1	2-1	2-2	3-3	5-1	6-2
Boston United	0-1		1-2	1-1	1-0	0-1	0-1	2-3	2-2	1-2	0-0	1-0	1-1	2-1	0-2	0-5	0-2	3-2	5-0	2-0	0-0	0-1
Bradford Park Avenue	6-4	1-1		1-0	1-2	0-2	2-0	1-0	2-2	3-0	0-1	2-2	2-1	2-0	3-2	0-0	3-1	2-0	4-0	3-2	0-2	1-1
Buxton	1-2	0-1	1-1		3-0	0-0	0-1	1-1	2-1	0-3	0-2	2-2	0-0	0-2	4-1	0-2	2-1	0-0	2-2	3-0	2-1	2-0
Cammell Laird	1-2	0-0	1-2	0-1		1-0	2-1	2-0	5-4	1-1	0-1	2-3	2-1	3-2	2-2	0-1	1-2	0-1	1-1	2-2	1-2	2-1
Eastwood Town	2-1	1-0	1-1	2-1	4-1		4-2	4-2	1-3	2-1	2-2	1-1	2-0	4-0	1-0	3-1	5-0	2-0	1-1	1-1	2-1	4-0
FC United of Manchester	4-0	0-1	1-1	1-1	5-5	0-1		2-0	2-1	3-0	3-1	1-3	2-4	3-2	3-3	0-0	4-0	3-2	2-0	3-1	5-3	0-0
Frickley Athletic	3-0	0-0	3-4	1-0	1-1	0-0	1-3		2-2	0-0	1-1	2-1	0-0	0-1	3-1	0-4	0-0	2-2	3-1	1-0	2-0	0-3
Guiseley	3-1	3-1	1-3	1-3	2-0	2-1	2-2	2-3		1-2	1-1	3-2	3-1	4-0	1-1	2-2	2-0	0-1	4-0	1-3	2-0	6-0
Hednesford Town	2-1	0-1	3-1	2-1	4-1	0-1	2-2	1-0	2-2		0-1	3-3	1-2	1-2	4-0	2-0	0-2	0-3	4-1	1-3	2-0	5-0
Ilkeston Town	2-1	1-1	0-0	1-0	2-1	1-0	0-1	1-0	0-1	0-1		1-1	3-1	5-0	2-2	3-2	1-0	2-1	3-0	1-0	3-1	3-3
Kendal Town	5-1	3-0	5-0	3-2	4-2	2-0	1-2	1-1	1-4	4-1	1-1		2-0	1-2	2-2	1-3	3-2	2-3	5-1	3-3	1-0	0-0
Leigh Genesis	3-0	0-0	2-1	0-7	2-1	0-4	0-2	2-0	2-4	1-3	1-2	1-2		0-0	0-2	0-8	0-3	0-6	2-1	2-4	0-2	1-2
Marine	1-1	3-1	0-4	2-0	0-0	1-2	2-3	1-2	2-0	0-3	0-2	0-1	0-1		2-1	0-0	1-0	2-1	3-6	2-2	0-2	6-2
Matlock Town	2-1	0-2	0-4	0-2	2-0	1-1	2-1	0-2	2-2	2-0	1-1	0-0	5-0	4-0		2-3	3-2	1-3	2-2	2-0	1-0	2-2
Nantwich Town	3-1	5-0	1-0	3-2	0-1	2-2	3-0	2-2	0-2	1-3	0-1	4-0	1-1	0-3	1-1		4-0	2-0	3-2	3-1	2-0	3-1
North Ferriby United	1-2	0-2	2-2	4-2	2-0	2-2	0-2	4-1	1-2	2-1	0-0	1-2	1-2	1-2	6-3	1-1		4-1	5-0	1-0	1-2	5-0
Ossett Town	3-1	0-0	1-2	1-1	2-2	0-3	0-4	2-0	1-4	1-1	1-3	5-1	0-2	4-5	3-2	2-1	0-1		1-1	6-2	4-2	1-0
Prescot Cables	1-1	2-2	1-1	2-0	1-4	1-5	4-3	0-2	3-6	0-5	0-2	0-1	2-0	1-2	2-2	2-0	1-2	2-3		2-4	1-3	0-1
Whitby Town	1-2	1-0	1-0	0-2	0-3	1-3	0-0	2-2	0-2	0-3	3-0	2-3	2-2	2-0	2-0	0-0	1-2	5-2	3-0		1-0	0-2
Witton Albion	4-2	1-2	1-4	4-1	2-3	1-2	2-1	1-1	1-2	0-2	2-0	1-3	1-3	1-3	2-0	0-2	2-1	1-1	0-0	0-0		2-3
Worksop Town	1-1	1-1	1-1	2-3	1-1	1-1	0-3	3-1	0-4	2-7	0-1	0-2	2-1	1-0	0-1	0-4	2-1	1-0	3-3	1-0	2-2	

Unibond League Premier Division

Season 2008/2009

Team	P	W	D	L	F	A	Pts
Eastwood Town	42	25	12	5	82	37	87
Ilkeston Town	42	23	13	6	59	34	82
Nantwich Town	42	22	10	10	83	41	76
Guiseley	42	22	10	10	98	60	76
Kendal Town	42	21	11	10	85	63	74
FC United of Manchester	42	21	9	12	82	58	72
Bradford Park Avenue	42	20	12	10	74	52	72
Hednesford Town	42	21	6	15	78	52	69
Ashton United	42	16	10	16	71	75	58
North Ferriby United	42	16	6	20	67	65	54
Frickley Athletic	42	13	15	14	50	58	54
Ossett Town	42	15	8	19	71	74	53
Marine	42	15	6	21	54	75	51
Buxton	42	13	10	19	56	58	49
Matlock Town	42	12	13	17	65	74	49
Boston United	42	12	13	17	38	52	49
Worksop Town	42	12	12	18	48	87	48
Cammell Laird	42	12	11	19	58	70	47
Whitby Town	42	12	10	20	58	71	46
Witton Albion	42	12	6	24	53	73	42
Leigh Genesis	42	11	7	24	42	88	40
Prescot Cables	42	5	12	25	52	107	27

Promotion Play-offs

Ilkeston Town 4   Kendal Town .... 3 (aet)
Nantwich Town 2   Guiseley .... 1 (aet)

Ilkeston Town 2   Nantwich Town .... 1 (aet)

Promoted: Eastwood Town and Ilkeston Town

Southern Premier League — Premier Division — 2008/2009 Season

	Banbury United	Bashley	Bedford Town	Brackley Town	Cambridge City	Chippenham Town	Clevedon Town	Corby Town	Evesham United	Farnborough	Gloucester City	Halesowen Town	Hemel Hempstead Town	Hitchin Town	Mangotsfield United	Merthyr Tydfil	Oxford City	Rugby Town	Stourbridge	Swindon Supermarine	Tiverton Town	Yate Town
Banbury United	■	1-0	4-0	3-1	2-2	0-5	3-1	0-4	0-6	0-2	1-5	2-1	3-0	1-4	1-1	1-1	1-0	2-1	2-0	1-5	0-3	3-0
Bashley	1-0	■	1-0	1-1	0-0	2-1	1-0	0-3	0-0	1-0	1-1	1-3	2-1	4-0	0-1	1-3	3-2	3-1	4-1	2-2	0-3	1-1
Bedford Town	3-0	0-2	■	0-0	1-1	2-0	0-0	1-5	1-1	0-2	1-1	1-0	1-2	5-0	3-1	1-0	3-1	2-0	2-1	1-0	1-1	1-1
Brackley Town	1-2	2-4	2-0	■	2-0	1-0	1-1	5-0	2-1	1-1	2-3	4-1	3-2	1-2	3-1	2-2	2-1	2-2	3-0	0-3	1-2	0-1
Cambridge City	3-1	5-0	1-0	1-0	■	0-1	0-1	3-2	2-3	0-2	2-1	3-0	1-0	3-1	0-2	3-0	1-0	3-2	2-0	0-1	1-0	2-2
Chippenham Town	1-0	2-3	1-0	3-1	3-1	■	2-1	3-1	1-0	1-1	2-2	2-1	1-2	1-1	1-1	1-0	0-2	1-1	1-2	3-1	1-0	3-0
Clevedon Town	1-1	0-0	2-1	2-2	1-0	3-2	■	1-3	2-0	1-1	1-4	1-2	0-3	1-2	2-3	1-5	0-1	1-0	2-0	1-2	1-2	4-3
Corby Town	5-0	3-1	1-2	2-0	0-0	3-0	4-0	■	0-0	3-1	1-2	1-2	0-0	2-0	1-1	2-1	0-1	2-0	0-0	2-1	1-4	1-1
Evesham United	2-0	2-2	0-1	1-1	0-1	2-0	0-0	1-1	■	0-0	2-2	0-0	4-1	2-1	3-1	0-2	0-1	1-0	0-1	1-0	1-1	4-1
Farnborough	1-0	1-1	3-1	2-2	1-1	2-0	3-1	3-3	2-1	■	2-1	1-1	1-0	1-0	3-1	0-1	0-2	2-1	4-0	1-0	1-0	2-0
Gloucester City	1-1	3-0	0-1	0-1	2-1	2-0	0-1	1-3	0-0		■	1-2	2-1	4-1	5-2	1-1	2-2	3-0	4-0	3-1	2-1	4-0
Halesowen Town	2-1	2-0	2-1	3-2	2-2	2-2	3-5	0-5	3-1	0-1	1-2	■	2-1	3-2	2-0	2-0	5-2	0-4	1-3	2-4	0-1	5-3
Hemel Hempstead Town	1-0	0-0	1-0	2-1	0-1	1-1	0-0	0-1	4-0	3-1	2-1	1-1	■	4-2	3-0	1-0	0-1	3-1	4-3	1-1	0-1	1-0
Hitchin Town	2-0	1-1	0-0	0-1	1-1	2-1	2-2	2-2	1-2	1-3	1-1	0-1	2-1	■	3-2	2-2	0-4	1-1	2-2	0-1	0-1	3-1
Mangotsfield United	1-0	1-0	3-2	0-3	0-3	0-4	2-0	0-3	0-0	0-2	0-1	0-1	0-1	2-1	■	0-3	2-2	0-2	1-2	2-1	3-2	1-2
Merthyr Tydfil	3-0	0-2	3-0	1-4	1-1	2-0	2-2	0-2	1-0	1-1	2-1	2-0	3-2	3-2	1-0	■	2-2	3-3	4-1	1-2	1-2	2-1
Oxford City	3-0	2-0	1-0	3-0	1-0	2-2	5-3	0-1	0-1	2-2	1-1	4-1	2-3	2-3	4-0	1-4	■	3-2	1-1	1-2	3-0	4-0
Rugby Town	0-0	2-3	3-0	3-3	2-3	0-1	4-0	0-2	0-1	2-3	1-3	0-2	0-5	4-3	2-1	3-0	1-1	■	4-0	0-0	2-0	2-2
Stourbridge	1-1	1-1	3-1	0-1	1-1	1-2	6-1	0-2	0-2	0-3	1-1	2-2	1-6	1-0	4-1	1-2	2-0	1-1	■	2-1	3-0	8-4
Swindon Supermarine	4-4	3-2	2-1	4-4	0-2	1-3	0-1	1-4	1-1	1-1	0-1	1-0	1-4	0-4	2-1	0-0	1-1	3-1	1-1	■	1-0	3-0
Tiverton Town	2-0	2-1	0-2	2-1	1-2	1-2	3-2	0-2	0-1	0-2	2-2	3-0	1-1	3-1	0-0	0-1	2-2	0-1	1-1	1-1	■	3-2
Yate Town	3-1	1-0	3-1	0-0	0-3	1-3	2-1	0-2	0-1	2-2	0-2	1-2	2-3	2-1	2-1	4-0	2-3	2-4	2-4	0-0	0-0	■

Southern League Premier Division

Season 2008/2009

	P	W	D	L	F	A	Pts
Corby Town	42	25	9	8	85	38	84
Farnborough	42	23	14	5	67	36	83
Gloucester City	42	21	12	9	80	45	75
Cambridge City	42	21	10	11	62	40	73
Hemel Hempstead Town	42	21	7	14	71	48	70
Oxford City	42	19	10	13	76	55	67
Merthyr Tydfil	42	19	10	13	66	55	67
Chippenham Town	42	20	8	14	64	51	65
Evesham United	42	16	13	13	48	39	61
Halesowen Town	42	19	6	17	65	73	60
Brackley Town	42	15	12	15	69	62	57
Tiverton Town	42	16	9	17	51	50	57
Swindon Supermarine	42	15	12	15	59	61	57
Bashley	42	15	12	15	52	58	57
Bedford Town	42	14	8	20	44	55	50
Stourbridge	42	13	11	18	62	78	50
Rugby Town	42	11	10	21	63	71	43
Clevedon Town	42	11	10	21	51	80	43
Banbury United	42	11	8	23	43	83	41
Hitchin Town	42	10	10	22	57	79	40
Yate Town	42	9	9	24	54	91	36
Mangotsfield United	42	10	6	26	39	80	36

Chippenham Town had 3 points deducted.
Halesowen Town had 3 points deducted.

Promotion Play-offs

Farnborough 0   Hemel Hempstead Town 0 (aet)
Farnborough won 4-3 on penalties
Gloucester City 3   Cambridge City 1

Farnborough 0   Gloucester City 1

Promoted: Corby Town and Gloucester City

Isthmian Football League Premier Division 2008/2009 Season	AFC Hornchurch	Ashford Town (Middlesex)	Billericay Town	Boreham Wood	Canvey Island	Carshalton Athletic	Dartford	Dover Athletic	Harlow Town	Harrow Borough	Hastings United	Hendon	Heybridge Swifts	Horsham	Maidstone United	Margate	Ramsgate	Staines Town	Sutton United	Tonbridge Angels	Tooting & Mitcham United	Wealdstone
AFC Hornchurch		1-3	1-1	1-4	1-0	0-2	2-0	1-0	3-1	2-0	1-2	1-2	2-3	3-0	0-0	3-0	3-0	0-2	2-1	3-0	1-0	1-0
Ashford Town (Middlesex)	2-0		5-1	0-1	1-0	1-1	1-0	1-2	0-2	0-0	5-4	0-2	0-1	3-0	1-0	0-1	0-3	2-0	2-1	1-7	7-0	2-1
Billericay Town	1-0	2-0		1-1	2-4	2-2	0-1	2-3	2-2	1-1	1-0	4-2	2-0	0-1	1-1	3-2	2-2	1-1	1-0	1-1	2-1	3-2
Boreham Wood	1-3	3-1	0-2		0-1	1-2	0-0	2-3	2-0	1-2	2-0	0-1	1-0	0-2	0-1	1-2	1-1	0-2	1-3	0-2	2-0	2-0
Canvey Island	3-2	1-0	4-0	4-0		0-1	2-3	0-3	1-3	3-1	5-2	1-1	2-0	2-4	0-1	0-4	2-0	2-2	0-0	3-2	3-1	1-1
Carshalton Athletic	2-2	1-0	3-1	0-2	2-2		0-2	0-1	3-1	2-3	2-2	1-0	0-0	1-5	0-3	2-1	3-3	1-3	0-2	0-3	0-1	3-2
Dartford	3-3	4-2	2-0	3-0	4-0	2-3		0-2	1-1	0-1	0-2	1-0	1-1	4-0	1-0	0-1	4-0	0-0	2-3	2-2	3-1	2-2
Dover Athletic	2-1	3-2	2-1	1-2	2-1	2-2	4-2		2-0	4-0	3-2	3-0	2-1	2-1	3-0	1-0	4-1	0-0	6-0	3-0	3-0	3-1
Harlow Town	4-1	2-5	3-0	3-3	3-0	1-2	1-2	1-4		3-0	0-1	3-5	0-1	0-1	2-3	1-1	1-1	0-2	1-1	0-2	0-2	2-0
Harrow Borough	1-2	0-1	3-1	1-1	2-4	1-5	2-1	3-0	1-4		1-1	4-2	0-0	6-1	1-1	3-2	0-1	2-1	0-0	2-3	0-0	0-3
Hastings United	2-4	1-2	5-2	1-1	2-0	0-1	0-0	0-1	3-2	0-2		2-1	0-1	0-2	0-4	1-1	3-1	1-1	0-2	0-1	0-3	2-1
Hendon	1-2	0-3	0-1	1-1	2-0	1-2	3-0	0-2	5-0	7-0	4-0		1-1	3-1	2-0	1-2	3-1	0-2	0-0	1-3	2-2	1-4
Heybridge Swifts	0-0	0-1	2-2	1-2	2-3	0-1	0-0	1-1	0-2	2-2	0-2	0-2		1-0	0-2	3-2	3-1	3-2	0-2	1-5	1-1	0-1
Horsham	0-0	2-0	0-1	2-2	3-0	2-3	0-3	1-2	1-4	1-0	0-2	1-2	2-0		3-1	2-0	1-0	2-1	1-2	0-0	0-0	0-2
Maidstone United	0-0	2-1	0-1	1-1	0-0	0-2	1-2	0-2	1-2	0-2	0-1	3-2	0-2	1-1		1-1	3-2	0-0	1-0	0-1	2-0	2-1
Margate	0-2	2-0	3-1	3-1	0-4	2-2	2-2	0-2	3-0	2-3	2-3	2-2	2-1	0-1	0-2		1-0	1-2	2-0	0-0	2-0	0-1
Ramsgate	1-2	0-3	1-0	2-0	2-2	1-2	0-1	0-0	1-2	0-2	0-1	1-5	3-2	2-2	1-2	2-0		1-1	3-1	2-3	1-4	2-2
Staines Town	2-2	3-0	1-0	4-1	2-1	4-1	2-1	2-3	1-0	1-0	2-0	2-0	3-2	0-0	3-1	4-1	2-0		3-1	2-2	0-0	2-2
Sutton United	2-1	3-1	0-1	1-1	1-0	1-1	1-0	1-0	3-0	2-2	2-1	1-0	1-1	2-1	2-2	2-0	1-1	1-1		3-3	0-0	3-2
Tonbridge Angels	0-1	3-2	3-2	1-1	3-0	1-0	4-1	0-2	2-0	1-1	3-3	5-1	2-1	4-0	2-2	1-0	2-2	1-2	1-3		0-2	1-2
Tooting & Mitcham United	2-0	3-2	0-0	1-2	3-1	1-2	0-2	1-1	4-2	1-1	1-0	1-0	2-3	0-2	2-0	2-1	3-0	1-2	4-2	2-2		2-3
Wealdstone	1-0	3-1	1-2	1-1	2-3	1-1	0-0	1-2	1-2	6-0	1-0	2-1	3-0	1-0	3-2	2-0	0-1	4-3	4-0	0-0	0-3	

Rymans League Premier Division

Season 2008/2009

Dover Athletic	42	33	5	4	91	34	104
Staines Town	42	23	13	6	75	41	82
Tonbridge Angels	42	20	13	9	82	54	73
Carshalton Athletic	42	19	11	12	64	63	68
Sutton United	42	18	13	11	57	53	67
AFC Hornchurch	42	19	8	15	60	51	65
Wealdstone	42	18	8	16	70	56	62
Dartford	42	17	11	14	62	49	62
Tooting & Mitcham United	42	16	10	16	57	57	58
Ashford Town (Middlesex)	42	18	2	22	64	66	56
Billericay Town	42	15	11	16	54	66	56
Canvey Island	42	16	7	19	65	70	55
Horsham	42	16	7	19	49	60	55
Harrow Borough	42	14	12	16	56	73	54
Maidstone United	42	14	11	17	46	51	53
Hendon	42	15	6	21	69	65	51
Hastings United	42	14	7	21	52	68	49
Boreham Wood	42	12	12	18	48	61	48
Margate	42	13	7	22	51	64	46
Harlow Town	42	13	6	23	61	77	42
Heybridge Swifts	42	10	11	21	41	63	41
Ramsgate	42	8	11	23	47	79	31

Harlow Town had 3 points deducted.
Ramsgate had 4 points deducted.

Promotion Play-offs

Staines Town	3	Sutton United	0
Tonbridge Angels	2	Carshalton Athletic	3
Staines Town	1	Carshalton Athletic	0

Promoted: Dover Athletic and Staines Town

F.A. Trophy 2008/2009

Qualifying 1	AFC Totton	3	Abingdon United	2
Qualifying 1	Andover	3	Gosport Borough	2
Qualifying 1	Ashton United	2	Lincoln United	1
Qualifying 1	Aveley	1	Hitchin Town	2
Qualifying 1	Banbury United	0	Burnham	1
Qualifying 1	Bedford Town	1	Corby Town	2
Qualifying 1	Boreham Wood	2	Burgess Hill Town	0
Qualifying 1	Boston United	6	Kidsgrove Athletic	0
Qualifying 1	Bracknell Town	2	Swindon Supermarine	4
Qualifying 1	Bradford Park Avenue	1	Clitheroe	2
Qualifying 1	Brentwood Town	2	AFC Sudbury	3
Qualifying 1	Brigg Town	1	Marine	5
Qualifying 1	Bromsgrove Rovers	1	Gloucester City	4
Qualifying 1	Bury Town	1	Leighton Town	0
Qualifying 1	Buxton	5	Carlton Town	3
Qualifying 1	Cambridge City	1	Canvey Island	1
Qualifying 1	Cheshunt	1	East Thurrock United	2
Qualifying 1	Chippenham Town	2	Fleet Town	1
Qualifying 1	Colwyn Bay	2	Chasetown	2
Qualifying 1	Concord Rangers	3	Billericay Town	1
Qualifying 1	Crowborough Athletic	0	Northwood	2
Qualifying 1	Dartford	2	Harlow Town	1
Qualifying 1	Durham City	4	Halesowen Town	4
Qualifying 1	Eastwood Town	0	Ilkeston Town	2
Qualifying 1	Enfield Town	0	Great Wakering Rovers	2
Qualifying 1	Evesham United	4	Clevedon Town	0
Qualifying 1	FC United of Manchester	1	Radcliffe Borough	0
Qualifying 1	Farnborough	4	Marlow	0
Qualifying 1	Frickley Athletic	0	Nantwich Town	2
Qualifying 1	Glapwell	3	Leamington	2
Qualifying 1	Guiseley	0	Ossett Town	1
Qualifying 1	Harrogate Railway Athletic	0	Leigh Genesis	1
Qualifying 1	Harrow Borough	2	Chatham Town	1
Qualifying 1	Hastings United	3	Carshalton Athletic	1
Qualifying 1	Hednesford Town	3	Quorn	1
Qualifying 1	Hemel Hempstead	6	AFC Hayes	0
Qualifying 1	Horsham	4	Sittingbourne	2
Qualifying 1	Lancaster City	3	Rugby Town	3
Qualifying 1	Maidstone United	1	AFC Hornchurch	1
Qualifying 1	Mangotsfield United	0	Bashley	2
Qualifying 1	Margate	0	Hendon	1
Qualifying 1	Matlock Town	0	Warrington Town	1
Qualifying 1	Merthyr Tydfil	4	Bishop's Cleeve	1
Qualifying 1	Metropolitan Police	0	Dulwich Hamlet	2
Qualifying 1	Newcastle Blue Star	2	Sutton Coldfield Town	2
Qualifying 1	Oxford City	3	Aylesbury United	1
Qualifying 1	Prescot Cables	0	Cammell Laird	3
Qualifying 1	Romulus	1	Garforth Town	1
Qualifying 1	Rushall Olympic	0	Bedworth United	0
Qualifying 1	Skelmersdale United	1	Sheffield	0
Qualifying 1	Soham Town Rangers	6	Witham Town	0
Qualifying 1	Spalding United	0	North Ferriby United	0
Qualifying 1	Staines Town	0	Dover Athletic	2
Qualifying 1	Stamford	3	Kendal Town	0

Qualifying 1	Stocksbridge Park Steels	3	Goole AFC	1	
Qualifying 1	Stourbridge	6	Salford City	0	
Qualifying 1	Sutton United	2	Tooting & Mitcham United	0	
Qualifying 1	Thatcham Town	5	Slough Town	4	
Qualifying 1	Tilbury	1	Cray Wanderers	1	
Qualifying 1	Tiverton Town	5	North Leigh	2	
Qualifying 1	Tonbridge Angels	2	Ramsgate	3	
Qualifying 1	Truro City	3	Chesham United	3	
Qualifying 1	Uxbridge	2	Walton & Hersham	1	
Qualifying 1	Walton Casuals	0	Heybridge Swifts	0	
Qualifying 1	Wealdstone	1	Croydon Athletic	0	
Qualifying 1	Whitby Town	3	Trafford	2	
Qualifying 1	Whitstable Town	3	Brackley Town	4	
Qualifying 1	Winchester City	0	Windsor & Eton	5	
Qualifying 1	Wingate & Finchley	1	Ashford Town (Middlesex)	1	
Qualifying 1	Witton Albion	0	Worksop Town	1	
Qualifying 1	Worthing	2	Merstham	0	
Qualifying 1	Yate Town	1	Stourport Swifts	1	
Replay	AFC Hornchurch	1	Maidstone United	2	
Replay	Ashford Town (Middlesex)	2	Wingate & Finchley	4	
Replay	Bedworth United	4	Rushall Olympic	1	
Replay	Canvey Island	0	Cambridge City	0	(aet)
	Cambridge City won on penalties				
Replay	Chasetown	2	Colwyn Bay	1	
Replay	Chesham United	2	Truro City	1	(aet)
Replay	Cray Wanderers	1	Tilbury	0	
Replay	Garforth Town	3	Romulus	4	
Replay	Halesowen Town	0	Durham City	1	
Replay	Heybridge Swifts	3	Walton Casuals	2	(aet)
Replay	North Ferriby United	2	Spalding United	0	
Replay	Rugby Town	2	Lancaster City	0	
Replay	Stourport Swifts	1	Yate Town	3	
Replay	Sutton Coldfield Town	4	Newcastle Blue Star	1	
Qualifying 2	Andover	3	Merthyr Tydfil	2	
Qualifying 2	Ashton United	0	Ilkeston Town	2	
Qualifying 2	Boreham Wood	1	Uxbridge	2	
Qualifying 2	Burnham	0	Windsor & Eton	5	
Qualifying 2	Buxton	0	Skelmersdale United	1	
Qualifying 2	Chasetown	1	North Ferriby United	1	
Qualifying 2	Clitheroe	2	Boston United	4	
Qualifying 2	Concord Rangers	1	Hemel Hempstead	3	
Qualifying 2	Corby Town	2	Chesham United	3	
Qualifying 2	Dartford	3	Oxford City	3	
Qualifying 2	Dover Athletic	2	Cambridge City	3	
Qualifying 2	Dulwich Hamlet	0	Bury Town	3	
Qualifying 2	East Thurrock United	4	Gloucester City	2	
Qualifying 2	Great Wakering Rovers	1	AFC Sudbury	1	
Qualifying 2	Harrow Borough	2	Hastings United	3	
Qualifying 2	Hendon	1	Sutton United	2	
Qualifying 2	Heybridge Swifts	0	Chippenham Town	0	
Qualifying 2	Hitchin Town	3	Ramsgate	6	
Qualifying 2	Horsham	1	Cray Wanderers	2	
Qualifying 2	Leigh Genesis	1	Cammell Laird	5	
Qualifying 2	Marine	1	Durham City	2	
Qualifying 2	Northwood	1	Brackley Town	4	
Qualifying 2	Ossett Town	1	Bedworth United	0	

Qualifying 2	Romulus	2	Warrington Town	2	
Qualifying 2	Rugby Town	1	Nantwich Town	3	
Qualifying 2	Soham Town Rangers	0	Farnborough	5	
Qualifying 2	Stamford	3	Hednesford Town	4	
Qualifying 2	Stocksbridge Park Steels	0	Whitby Town	2	
Qualifying 2	Stourbridge	2	Evesham United	1	
Qualifying 2	Sutton Coldfield Town	2	Glapwell	3	
Qualifying 2	Swindon Supermarine	2	Maidstone United	0	
Qualifying 2	Thatcham Town	0	AFC Totton	4	
Qualifying 2	Wealdstone	1	Tiverton Town	2	
Qualifying 2	Wingate & Finchley	1	Worthing	0	
Qualifying 2	Worksop Town	0	FC United of Manchester	3	
Qualifying 2	Yate Town	1	Bashley	3	
Replay	AFC Sudbury	4	Great Wakering Rovers	3	(aet)
Replay	Chippenham Town	0	Heybridge Swifts	1	
Replay	North Ferriby United	1	Chasetown	4	
Replay	Oxford City	2	Dartford	4	
Replay	Warrington Town	3	Romulus	1	(aet)
Qualifying 3	Andover	0	Newport County	3	
Qualifying 3	Basingstoke Town	1	Thurrock	0	
Qualifying 3	Bath City	5	East Thurrock United	1	
Qualifying 3	Bishop's Stortford	0	Tiverton Town	0	
Qualifying 3	Blyth Spartans	3	Alfreton Town	4	
Qualifying 3	Braintree Town	1	Farnborough	1	
Qualifying 3	Cambridge City	1	Hastings United	0	
Qualifying 3	Chasetown	1	Ilkeston Town	2	
Qualifying 3	Cray Wanderers	0	Brackley Town	3	
Qualifying 3	Eastleigh	0	Bashley	2	
Qualifying 3	FC United of Manchester	1	Boston United	3	
Qualifying 3	Farsley Celtic	2	Droylsden	0	
Qualifying 3	Fisher Athletic	0	Havant & Waterlooville	2	
Qualifying 3	Gainsborough Trinity	0	AFC Telford United	2	
Qualifying 3	Gateshead	0	Harrogate Town	2	
Qualifying 3	Glapwell	0	Skelmersdale United	1	
Qualifying 3	Hampton & Richmond Borough	1	Bury Town	2	
Qualifying 3	Hayes & Yeading United	4	Chelmsford City	1	
Qualifying 3	Hemel Hempstead	5	Heybridge Swifts	1	
Qualifying 3	Hinckley United	1	Burscough	2	
Qualifying 3	Hyde United	1	Hednesford Town	1	
Qualifying 3	King's Lynn	3	Stafford Rangers	2	
Qualifying 3	Maidenhead United	2	Chesham United	4	
Qualifying 3	Ossett Town	3	Fleetwood Town	1	
Qualifying 3	Ramsgate	0	Bognor Regis Town	2	
Qualifying 3	Redditch United	1	Cammell Laird	1	
Qualifying 3	Solihull Moors	1	Durham City	2	
Qualifying 3	St Albans City	0	Dartford	0	
Qualifying 3	Stourbridge	3	Hucknall Town	2	
Qualifying 3	Swindon Supermarine	1	Bromley	0	
Qualifying 3	Tamworth	0	Workington	1	
Qualifying 3	Team Bath	2	Windsor & Eton	1	
Qualifying 3	Uxbridge	2	Dorchester Town	1	
Qualifying 3	Vauxhall Motors (Cheshire)	0	Southport	0	
Qualifying 3	Warrington Town	0	Nantwich Town	1	
Qualifying 3	Welling United	1	AFC Totton	1	
Qualifying 3	Weston Super Mare	1	AFC Sudbury	2	
Qualifying 3	Whitby Town	0	Stalybridge Celtic	3	

Qualifying 3	Wingate & Finchley	1	Sutton United	1	
Qualifying 3	Worcester City	1	AFC Wimbledon	3	
Replay	AFC Totton	1	Welling United	2	
Replay	Cammell Laird	0	Redditch United	2	
Replay	Dartford	1	St Albans City	1	(aet)
	St. Albans City won on penalties				
Replay	Farnborough	6	Braintree Town	2	
Replay	Hednesford Town	5	Hyde United	0	
Replay	Southport	2	Vauxhall Motors (Cheshire)	1	
Replay	Sutton United	2	Wingate & Finchley	2	(aet)
	Wingate & Finchley won on penalties				
Replay	Tiverton Town	1	Bishop's Stortford	0	
Round 1	AFC Sudbury	0	Oxford United	2	
Round 1	Alfreton Town	0	Redditch United	1	
Round 1	Altrincham	1	Southport	4	
Round 1	Barrow	2	Skelmersdale United	1	
Round 1	Bashley	2	Tiverton Town	2	
Round 1	Basingstoke Town	3	Brackley Town	1	
Round 1	Bognor Regis Town	0	Ebbsfleet United	2	
Round 1	Boston United	1	AFC Telford United	2	
Round 1	Burton Albion	1	Farsley Celtic	1	
Round 1	Cambridge City	1	Kettering Town	4	
Round 1	Chesham United	2	Crawley Town	4	
Round 1	Durham City	2	Harrogate Town	0	
Round 1	Farnborough	3	Wingate & Finchley	1	
Round 1	Forest Green Rovers	5	Hemel Hempstead	1	
Round 1	Havant & Waterlooville	3	Bury Town	1	
Round 1	Hayes & Yeading United	2	Grays Athletic	0	
Round 1	Hednesford Town	3	Nantwich Town	2	
Round 1	Histon	2	Cambridge United	3	
Round 1	Ilkeston Town	3	Ossett Town	2	
Round 1	Kidderminster Harriers	3	Burscough	2	
Round 1	Newport County	1	Rushden & Diamonds	1	
Round 1	Northwich Victoria	0	York City	2	
Round 1	Stevenage Borough	4	St Albans City	1	
Round 1	Stourbridge	1	Stalybridge Celtic	6	
Round 1	Swindon Supermarine	1	Eastbourne Borough	0	
Round 1	Team Bath	1	Lewes	2	
Round 1	Torquay United	2	Bath City	0	
Round 1	Uxbridge	2	AFC Wimbledon	1	
Round 1	Welling United	2	Weymouth	0	
Round 1	Woking	1	Salisbury City	2	
Round 1	Workington	4	King's Lynn	3	
Round 1	Wrexham	2	Mansfield Town	1	
Replay	Farsley Celtic	2	Burton Albion	2	(aet)
	Burton Albion won on penalties				
Replay	Rushden & Diamonds	1	Newport County	1	(aet)
	Rushden & Diamonds won on penalties				
Replay	Tiverton Town	2	Bashley	1	
Round 2	AFC Telford United	4	Hayes & Yeading United	0	
Round 2	Barrow	0	Workington	3	
Round 2	Basingstoke Town	1	Wrexham	2	
Round 2	Burton Albion	3	Salisbury City	0	
Round 2	Cambridge United	0	Crawley Town	5	
Round 2	Durham City	1	Southport	1	
Round 2	Ebbsfleet United	2	Stalybridge Celtic	1	

Round 2	Farnborough	0	Stevenage Borough	2	
Round 2	Forest Green Rovers	5	Redditch United	0	
Round 2	Hednesford Town	4	Welling United	3	
Round 2	Ilkeston Town	3	Kidderminster Harriers	5	
Round 2	Lewes	3	Havant & Waterlooville	3	
Round 2	Oxford United	1	York City	2	
Round 2	Tiverton Town	1	Kettering Town	1	
Round 2	Torquay United	1	Rushden & Diamonds	0	
Round 2	Uxbridge	1	Swindon Supermarine	6	
Replay	Havant & Waterlooville	4	Lewes	3	
Replay	Kettering Town	1	Tiverton Town	1	(aet)
	Kettering Town won on penalties				
Replay	Southport	3	Durham City	1	
Round 3	Ebbsfleet United	2	Swindon Supermarine	0	
Round 3	Forest Green Rovers	1	Hednesford Town	0	
Round 3	Havant & Waterlooville	2	Crawley Town	0	
Round 3	Kettering Town	0	AFC Telford United	1	
Round 3	Kidderminster Harriers	1	York City	1	
Round 3	Southport	3	Torquay United	0	
Round 3	Stevenage Borough	4	Burton Albion	0	
Round 3	Workington	1	Wrexham	3	
Replay	York City	1	Kidderminster Harriers	1	(aet)
	York City won on penalties				
Round 4	AFC Telford United	2	Southport	2	
Round 4	Stevenage Borough	4	Forest Green Rovers	0	
Round 4	Wrexham	0	Ebbsfleet United	0	
Round 4	York City	2	Havant & Waterlooville	0	
Replay	Ebbsfleet United	3	Wrexham	1	
Replay	Southport	0	AFC Telford United	1	
Semi-finals					
1st leg	AFC Telford United	0	York City	2	
2nd leg	York City	2	AFC Telford United	1	
	York City won 4-1 on aggregate				
1st leg	Stevenage Borough	3	Ebbsfleet United	2	
2nd leg	Ebbsfleet United	0	Stevenage Borough	1	
	Stevenage Borough won 4-2 on aggregate				
FINAL	Stevenage Borough	2	York City	0	

F.A. Vase 2008/2009

Round 1	Almondsbury Town	1	Reading Town	0	
Round 1	Alsager Town	2	Hallam	2	(aet)
Round 1	Alvechurch	1	Causeway United	3	(aet)
Round 1	Arundel	1	Chertsey Town	0	
Round 1	Ashington	3	Leeds Carnegie	1	
Round 1	Ashton Athletic	2	Nostell MW	2	(aet)
Round 1	Aylesbury Vale	5	Harrow Hill	1	
Round 1	Banstead Athletic	2	Erith & Belvedere	1	
Round 1	Barkingside	2	Bowers & Pitsea	2	(aet)
Round 1	Barnstaple Town	1	Hamworthy United	2	
Round 1	Bartley Green	1	Barwell	2	
Round 1	Basildon United	4	Stotfold	1	
Round 1	Bedlington Terriers	1	Stokesley SC	1	(aet)
Round 1	Bemerton Heath Harlequins	3	Shortwood United	0	
Round 1	Biggleswade Town	2	Berkhamsted Town	0	
Round 1	Biggleswade United	3	Desborough Town	0	
Round 1	Bootle	2	Ramsbottom United	1	(aet)
Round 1	Borrowash Victoria	1	Arnold Town	3	
Round 1	Bridlington Town	6	West Allotment Celtic	1	
Round 1	Brislington	3	Bodmin Town	2	
Round 1	Buckingham Town	2	Malmesbury Victoria	0	
Round 1	Castle Vale	1	Stone Dominoes	2	
Round 1	Chalfont St Peter	5	Totton & Eling	2	
Round 1	Chessington & Hook United	0	Shoreham	3	
Round 1	Chichester City United	2	Epsom & Ewell	0	
Round 1	Coalville Town	4	Newark Town	0	
Round 1	Cogenhoe United	6	Codicote	0	
Round 1	Colne	2	Abbey Hey	3	
Round 1	Cornard United	2	Wisbech Town	0	
Round 1	Cove	1	Christchurch	2	
Round 1	Crook Town	2	Shildon	4	
Round 1	Cullompton Rangers	0	Willand Rovers	0	(aet)
	The result of this game was declared null and void and a replay was ordered:				
Round 1	Cullompton Rangers	0	Willand Rovers	1	(aet)
Round 1	Darlaston	3	Eccleshall	1	
Round 1	Daventry Town	2	Daventry United	0	
Round 1	Dawlish Town	5	Launceston	1	
Round 1	Dereham Town	4	Newmarket Town	2	
Round 1	Dosthill Colts	2	Loughborough University	1	
Round 1	Dudley Town	2	Rothley Imperial	0	
Round 1	East Grinstead Town	4	Rye United	2	
Round 1	East Preston	0	Whitehawk	2	
Round 1	Esh Winning	1	Scarborough Athletic	2	
Round 1	Eton Manor	1	Sport London E Benfica	2	
Round 1	FC Clacton	4	Bedfont Green	1	
Round 1	Fareham Town	0	Binfield	0	(aet)
Round 1	Flackwell Heath	1	Hook Norton	6	
Round 1	Frimley Green	2	Redhill	1	
Round 1	Frome Town	2	Tavistock	1	(aet)
Round 1	Guildford City	1	Selsey	3	
Round 1	Guisborough Town	1	Ryton	1	(aet)
Round 1	Hadleigh United	0	Debenham LC	1	
Round 1	Halstead Town	2	Raunds Town	4	
Round 1	Hayling United	3	Brading Town	0	

Round 1	Holbeach United	1	Felixstowe & Walton United	1	(aet)
Round 1	Horley Town	2	Croydon	4	
Round 1	Horsham YMCA	1	Peacehaven & Telscombe	4	
Round 1	Hythe Town	0	Egham Town	3	
Round 1	Kentish Town	5	Thrapston Town	2	
Round 1	Kirby Muxloe	1	Pilkington XXX	3	
Round 1	Leek CSOB	1	Boldmere St Michaels	2	
Round 1	Leverstock Green	2	Northampton Spencer	3	
Round 1	Long Melford	0	St Neots Town	2	
Round 1	Longwell Green Sports	0	Clanfield 85	1	
Round 1	Lordswood	1	St Francis Rangers	5	
Round 1	Maine Road	3	Runcorn Linnets	3	
Round 1	Market Drayton Town	3	Teversal	0	
Round 1	Melksham Town	0	New Milton Town	1	(aet)
Round 1	Mildenhall Town	4	Diss Town	2	
Round 1	Mile Oak	1	Cobham	0	
Round 1	Molesey	2	Badshot Lea	1	
Round 1	New Mills	1	Glossop North End	4	
Round 1	Newcastle Benfield	4	Peterlee Town	1	
Round 1	Newcastle Town	5	Highgate United	0	
Round 1	Newport (IOW)	0	Witney United	1	
Round 1	Oldham Town	1	Congleton Town	0	
Round 1	Penrith	2	Squires Gate	1	
Round 1	Porthleven	1	Larkhall Athletic	2	
Round 1	Potton United	1	Wivenhoe Town	3	
Round 1	Racing Club Warwick	1	Heanor Town	2	(aet)
Round 1	Rainworth MW	1	Dunkirk	3	
Round 1	Rossington Main	1	Brodsworth MW	4	
Round 1	Royston Town	1	Wellingborough Town	3	(aet)
Round 1	Sandhurst Town	2	Warminster Town	1	
Round 1	Shaftesbury	0	Wimborne Town	3	
Round 1	Sherborne Town	2	Saltash United	4	
Round 1	Shifnal Town	0	Biddulph Victoria	1	
Round 1	St Margaretsbury	1	Romford	2	
Round 1	Stewarts & Lloyds	3	Oxhey Jets	0	
Round 1	Stratford Town	6	Coleshill Town	0	
Round 1	Street	1	Clevedon United	1	(aet)
Round 1	Sunderland Nissan	0	Morpeth Town	0	(aet)
Round 1	Sunderland RCA	1	Marske United	2	
Round 1	Tadcaster Albion	1	Spennymoor Town	5	
Round 1	Thackley	3	Liversedge	0	
Round 1	Tiptree United	8	Hertford Town	0	
Round 1	Tunbridge Wells	4	Ash United	1	
Round 1	VT	6	Calne Town	1	
Round 1	Warstones Wanderers	0	Long Eaton United	4	
Round 1	Westfields	2	Lye Town	1	
Round 1	Winterton Rangers	2	Selby Town	1	
Round 1	Wootton Bassett Town	3	Kidlington	2	
Round 1	Wroxham	0	Leiston	2	
Round 1	Yaxley	3	Kirkley & Pakefield	3	(aet)
Replay	Binfield	3	Fareham Town	2	
Replay	Bowers & Pitsea	0	Barkingside	2	
Replay	Clevedon United	2	Street	4	
Replay	Felixstowe & Walton United	0	Holbeach United	1	
Replay	Hallam	1	Alsager Town	3	
Replay	Kirkley & Pakefield	5	Yaxley	1	

Replay	Morpeth Town	3	Sunderland Nissan	4	(aet)
Replay	Nostell MW	3	Ashton Athletic	1	
Replay	Runcorn Linnets	2	Maine Road	1	(aet)
Replay	Ryton	10	Guisborough Town	0	
Replay	Stokesley SC	3	Bedlington Terriers	1	(aet)
Round 2	AFC Fylde	1	Newcastle Benfield	0	
Round 2	Almondsbury Town	0	Hungerford Town	2	
Round 2	Alsager Town	1	Runcorn Linnets	1	(aet)
Round 2	Arnold Town	4	Pilkington XXX	0	
Round 2	Aylesbury Vale	4	East Grinstead Town	0	
Round 2	Banstead Athletic	1	Arundel	2	(aet)
Round 2	Barwell	3	Studley	3	(aet)
Round 2	Biggleswade United	0	Stanway Rovers	3	
Round 2	Bitton	4	Poole Town	2	
Round 2	Blackstones	2	Dunkirk	0	
Round 2	Bootle	5	Oldham Town	3	
Round 2	Boston Town	1	Cogenhoe United	2	
Round 2	Bridlington Town	0	Penrith	2	
Round 2	Brislington	2	Bideford	4	
Round 2	Brodsworth MW	0	Pickering Town	2	
Round 2	Camberley Town	4	Peacehaven & Telscombe	3	(aet)
Round 2	Chalfont St Peter	2	Clanfield 85	0	
Round 2	Chichester City United	0	Shoreham	4	(aet)
Round 2	Christchurch	1	Tunbridge Wells	0	
Round 2	Consett	0	Marske United	1	
Round 2	Croydon	3	Mile Oak	0	
Round 2	Darlaston	0	Long Eaton United	3	
Round 2	Daventry Town	3	Dudley Town	1	
Round 2	Dawlish Town	3	Street	4	
Round 2	Dosthill Colts	2	Coalville Town	5	
Round 2	Egham Town	0	Buckingham Town	1	
Round 2	FC Clacton	4	Basildon United	0	
Round 2	Formby	0	Dunston Federation	4	
Round 2	Frimley Green	1	Binfield	0	
Round 2	Frome Town	4	Saltash United	1	
Round 2	Glossop North End	4	Biddulph Victoria	0	
Round 2	Harefield United	2	Barkingside	1	
Round 2	Hayling United	2	New Milton Town	4	
Round 2	Hook Norton	1	VT	1	(aet)
Round 2	Kentish Town	2	Biggleswade Town	6	(aet)
Round 2	Kirkley & Pakefield	0	Dereham Town	1	
Round 2	Larkhall Athletic	4	Lymington Town	1	
Round 2	Leiston	1	Debenham LC	0	
Round 2	Lowestoft Town	2	Tiptree United	0	
Round 2	Market Drayton Town	2	Newcastle Town	1	
Round 2	Molesey	3	St Francis Rangers	0	
Round 2	Needham Market	1	Northampton Spencer	0	
Round 2	Raunds Town	1	Holbeach United	2	(aet)
Round 2	Ryton	2	Nostell MW	2	(aet)
Round 2	Sandhurst Town	1	Witney United	2	
Round 2	Scarborough Athletic	3	Sunderland Nissan	2	(aet)
Round 2	Selsey	2	Whitehawk	0	
Round 2	Shawbury United	2	Westfields	2	(aet)
Round 2	Shrivenham	2	Hamworthy United	2	(aet)
Round 2	Spennymoor Town	2	Stokesley SC	1	
Round 2	Sport London E Benfica	0	St Neots Town	5	

89

Round 2	St Ives Town	2	Romford	1	
Round 2	Stewarts & Lloyds	5	Heanor Town	1	
Round 2	Stone Dominoes	1	Coventry Sphinx	0	
Round 2	Stratford Town	4	Causeway United	2	
Round 2	Thackley	0	Shildon	1	
Round 2	Tipton Town	1	Boldmere St Michaels	0	
Round 2	VCD Athletic	2	Mildenhall Town	1	
Round 2	Wellingborough Town	0	Long Buckby	3	
Round 2	Whitley Bay	5	Abbey Hey	2	(aet)
Round 2	Willand Rovers	2	Bemerton Heath Harlequins	1	(aet)
Round 2	Wimborne Town	4	Wootton Bassett Town	0	
Round 2	Winterton Rangers	3	Ashington	1	(aet)
Round 2	Wivenhoe Town	3	Cornard United	0	
Replay	Hamworthy United	4	Shrivenham	1	
Replay	Nostell MW	4	Ryton	1	
Replay	Runcorn Linnets	2	Alsager Town	2	(aet)
	Runcorn Linnets won on penalties				
Replay	Studley	2	Barwell	2	(aet)
	Barwell won on penalties				
Replay	Westfields	2	Shawbury United	2	(aet)
	Westfields won on penalties				
Round 3	AFC Fylde	4	Runcorn Linnets	1	
Round 3	Arundel	1	Cogenhoe United	4	
Round 3	Barwell	0	Coalville Town	1	
Round 3	Bideford	2	Frome Town	1	
Round 3	Biggleswade Town	6	Wivenhoe Town	0	
Round 3	Christchurch	3	New Milton Town	0	
Round 3	Croydon	3	Camberley Town	1	
Round 3	Dereham Town	3	Molesey	1	(aet)
Round 3	FC Clacton	4	Holbeach United	3	(aet)
Round 3	Frimley Green	1	VCD Athletic	1	(aet)
Round 3	Glossop North End	2	Winterton Rangers	1	
Round 3	Hamworthy United	1	Hungerford Town	3	
Round 3	Larkhall Athletic	3	Wimborne Town	1	
Round 3	Leiston	4	Aylesbury Vale	1	
Round 3	Long Buckby	1	St Ives Town	2	(aet)
Round 3	Long Eaton United	0	Bootle	1	
Round 3	Lowestoft Town	2	Harefield United	1	
Round 3	Market Drayton Town	1	Arnold Town	1	(aet)
Round 3	Marske United	7	Pickering Town	0	
Round 3	Needham Market	4	St Neots Town	3	
Round 3	Penrith	0	Whitley Bay	1	(aet)
Round 3	Scarborough Athletic	6	Blackstones	1	
Round 3	Selsey	0	Chalfont St Peter	2	
Round 3	Spennymoor Town	3	Shildon	2	
Round 3	Stanway Rovers	1	Shoreham	0	
Round 3	Stewarts & Lloyds	2	Daventry Town	1	
Round 3	Stone Dominoes	1	Nostell MW	0	
Round 3	Stratford Town	1	Westfields	1	(aet)
Round 3	Street	0	Bitton	0	(aet)
Round 3	Tipton Town	0	Dunston Federation	3	
Round 3	VT	1	Willand Rovers	0	(aet)
Round 3	Witney United	2	Buckingham Town	1	
Replay	Arnold Town	0	Market Drayton Town	2	
Replay	Bitton	2	Street	1	(aet)

Replay	VCD Athletic	4	Frimley Green	0	
Replay	Westfields	0	Stratford Town	1	
Round 4	Bideford	1	Scarborough Athletic	0	
Round 4	Biggleswade Town	2	Croydon	1	
Round 4	Bitton	2	Cogenhoe United	1	
Round 4	Bootle	1	Whitley Bay	3	
Round 4	Christchurch	4	FC Clacton	0	
Round 4	Coalville Town	1	Spennymoor Town	1	(aet)
Round 4	Dunston Federation	5	Chalfont St Peter	6	(aet)
Round 4	Glossop North End	2	Stewarts & Lloyds	1	
Round 4	Hungerford Town	3	Leiston	2	(aet)
Round 4	Larkhall Athletic	2	Dereham Town	4	
Round 4	Lowestoft Town	1	Witney United	0	
Round 4	Market Drayton Town	2	VT	1	
Round 4	Needham Market	0	AFC Fylde	0	(aet)
Round 4	St Ives Town	0	Stanway Rovers	0	
Round 4	Stratford Town	3	Stone Dominoes	2	(aet)
Round 4	VCD Athletic	2	Marske United	3	
Replay	AFC Fylde	1	Needham Market	2	
Replay	Spennymoor Town	1	Coalville Town	1	(aet)
	Spennymoor Town won on penalties				
Replay	Stanway Rovers	0	St Ives Town	2	
Round 5	Bideford	2	Spennymoor Town	0	
Round 5	Biggleswade Town	4	Market Drayton Town	2	
Round 5	Bitton	0	Glossop North End	2	
Round 5	Chalfont St Peter	4	Christchurch	0	
Round 5	Lowestoft Town	4	Hungerford Town	3	(aet)
Round 5	Needham Market	2	Dereham Town	1	
Round 5	St Ives Town	0	Marske United	3	
Round 5	Whitley Bay	2	Stratford Town	0	
Round 6	Glossop North End	5	Marske United	2	
Round 6	Lowestoft Town	4	Bideford	0	
Round 6	Needham Market	1	Chalfont St Peter	1	(aet)
Round 6	Whitley Bay	5	Biggleswade Town	2	
Replay	Chalfont St Peter	0	Needham Market	0	(aet)
	Chalfont St Peter won on penalties				

Semi-finals

1st leg	Chalfont St Peter	3	Glossop North End	3	
2nd leg	Glossop North End	2	Chalfont St Peter	2	(aet)
	Aggregate 5-5. Glossop North End won on penalties				
1st leg	Whitley Bay	2	Lowestoft Town	1	
2nd leg	Lowestoft Town	1	Whitley Bay	1	
	Whitley Bay won 3-2 on aggregate				
FINAL	Whitley Bay	2	Glossop North End	0	

Cup Statistics provided by:

www.soccerdata.com

Football Conference Blue Square Premier Fixtures 2009/2010 Season	AFC Wimbledon	Altrincham	Barrow	Cambridge United	Chester City	Crawley Town	Eastbourne Borough	Ebbsfleet United	Forest Green Rovers	Gateshead	Grays Athletic	Hayes & Yeading United	Histon	Kettering Town	Kidderminster Harriers	Luton Town	Mansfield Town	Oxford United	Rushden & Diamonds	Salisbury City	Stevenage Borough	Tamworth	Wrexham	York City
AFC Wimbledon	■	06/03	30/01	12/09	17/04	22/09	13/03	24/11	06/02	05/12	19/01	26/12	26/09	17/10	03/10	08/08	16/01	29/08	27/03	18/08	05/04	20/02	08/09	21/11
Altrincham	22/08	■	01/12	24/04	31/08	12/09	19/12	08/08	14/11	29/09	27/02	23/01	18/08	28/11	03/04	17/10	10/10	10/04	20/03	06/02	30/01	22/09	01/01	28/12
Barrow	14/11	11/08	■	06/03	05/04	20/03	27/03	17/10	19/09	26/12	24/11	05/12	16/01	13/02	20/02	06/02	29/09	03/10	05/09	17/04	15/08	29/08	19/01	08/09
Cambridge United	13/02	08/09	08/08	■	01/12	18/08	16/01	10/10	05/09	29/08	27/03	17/04	13/03	14/11	31/10	26/09	05/04	19/12	24/11	16/03	26/12	27/02	19/09	23/01
Chester City	31/10	21/11	28/12	15/08	■	24/04	28/11	06/02	29/09	11/08	30/01	13/03	05/09	10/04	01/01	05/12	29/08	27/02	10/10	19/01	19/09	08/09	13/02	03/04
Crawley Town	19/12	13/02	10/10	06/02	16/01	■	26/12	13/03	11/08	22/08	29/08	05/04	08/09	19/09	23/01	27/02	14/11	01/12	26/09	24/11	27/03	17/04	15/08	31/10
Eastbourne Borough	11/08	20/02	22/08	05/12	12/09	01/01	■	31/08	03/04	30/01	20/03	22/09	24/11	03/10	06/03	28/12	17/10	24/04	15/08	14/11	19/01	26/09	06/02	10/04
Ebbsfleet United	19/09	16/01	27/02	11/08	27/03	03/10	05/04	■	23/01	17/04	26/12	29/08	19/12	09/02	15/08	20/03	28/11	05/09	08/09	29/09	01/12	21/11	31/10	13/02
Forest Green Rovers	10/10	27/03	13/03	20/02	09/02	19/01	31/10	12/09	■	16/01	26/09	08/09	17/04	08/08	22/09	18/08	30/01	24/11	05/12	26/12	21/11	05/04	29/08	06/03
Gateshead	24/04	02/02	01/01	03/04	17/10	28/11	10/10	20/02	27/02	■	21/11	05/09	08/08	19/12	10/04	23/01	01/12	26/09	22/09	12/09	20/03	18/08	28/12	31/08
Grays Athletic	31/08	19/09	31/10	29/09	08/08	28/12	18/08	01/01	24/04	03/10	■	23/02	01/12	03/04	22/08	14/11	05/09	23/01	06/02	13/02	13/03	28/11	10/04	19/12
Hayes & Yeading Utd.	01/01	15/08	10/04	17/10	03/10	21/11	01/12	28/12	28/11	13/02	09/02	■	19/09	29/09	19/12	06/03	27/02	03/04	30/01	31/08	11/08	12/09	24/04	22/08
Histon	03/04	05/12	24/04	03/10	20/02	10/04	29/09	22/09	17/10	06/03	11/08	06/02	■	28/12	12/09	01/01	20/03	15/08	19/01	22/08	31/08	30/01	21/11	28/11
Kettering Town	15/08	05/09	22/09	19/01	06/03	30/01	17/04	26/09	20/03	08/09	20/02	24/11	05/04	■	21/11	29/08	27/03	11/08	16/01	05/12	31/10	26/12	10/10	06/02
Kidderminster Harriers	09/02	29/08	28/11	30/01	26/12	17/10	05/09	19/01	13/02	19/09	16/01	08/08	27/02	18/08	■	10/10	08/09	14/11	05/04	27/03	17/04	01/12	29/09	13/03
Luton Town	28/11	17/04	12/09	21/11	22/08	01/09	13/02	30/01	19/12	15/08	05/04	27/03	26/12	01/12	16/03	■	11/08	09/02	31/10	16/01	29/09	03/10	13/03	19/09
Mansfield Town	10/04	19/01	18/08	28/12	23/01	08/08	21/11	22/08	03/10	06/02	05/12	26/09	31/10	31/08	24/04	24/11	■	22/09	20/02	06/03	12/09	13/03	03/04	01/01
Oxford United	23/02	31/10	21/11	28/11	18/08	29/09	19/09	05/12	31/08	27/03	10/10	08/12	13/02	13/03	06/02	08/09	17/04	■	26/12	05/04	22/08	16/01	30/01	08/08
Rushden & Diamonds	29/09	03/10	23/01	31/08	19/12	03/04	09/02	10/04	22/08	13/03	12/09	18/08	14/11	27/02	28/12	24/04	19/09	01/01	■	08/08	13/02	17/10	28/11	01/12
Salisbury City	01/12	13/03	26/09	10/04	22/09	09/02	29/08	03/04	01/01	31/10	08/09	20/02	23/01	24/04	11/08	05/09	15/08	28/12	21/11	■	28/11	19/12	27/02	10/10
Stevenage Borough	28/12	26/09	19/12	01/01	24/11	06/03	08/09	18/08	10/04	14/11	22/09	10/10	16/03	23/01	05/12	03/04	09/02	20/02	29/08	17/10	■	08/08	05/09	24/04
Tamworth	05/09	24/11	03/04	22/08	14/11	05/12	23/01	24/04	28/12	19/01	15/08	31/10	10/10	01/01	31/08	10/04	13/02	20/03	06/03	19/09	06/02	■	11/08	29/09
Wrexham	23/01	26/12	31/08	20/03	26/09	20/02	08/08	06/03	01/12	05/04	17/10	14/11	27/03	22/08	24/11	22/09	19/12	12/09	17/04	03/10	16/01	09/02	■	18/08
York City	20/03	05/04	09/02	22/09	23/02	05/09	27/03	14/11	15/08	24/11	17/04	16/01	29/08	12/09	26/09	19/01	26/12	17/10	11/08	30/01	03/10	27/03	05/12	■

Please note that the above fixtures may be subject to change.

Football Conference Blue Square North Fixtures 2009/2010 Season	AFC Telford United	Alfreton Town	Blyth Spartans	Corby Town	Droylsden	Eastwood Town	Farsley Celtic	Fleetwood Town	Gainsborough Trinity	Gloucester City	Harrogate Town	Hinckley United	Hyde United	Ilkeston Town	Northwich Victoria	Redditch United	Solihull Moors	Southport	Stafford Rangers	Stalybridge Celtic	Vauxhall Motors	Workington
AFC Telford United		01/12	08/08	17/04	03/10	30/01	16/01	05/12	09/01	05/04	05/09	18/08	27/03	29/08	08/09	13/02	06/03	17/10	26/12	20/03	14/11	31/10
Alfreton Town	12/09		20/03	31/08	01/01	28/12	20/02	28/11	27/10	06/03	06/02	24/04	05/12	24/10	10/04	03/04	11/08	22/08	07/11	19/09	15/08	16/01
Blyth Spartans	27/02	03/10		22/08	31/08	14/11	28/12	17/04	30/01	27/03	01/12	17/10	03/04	31/10	06/03	15/08	12/09	11/08	13/02	19/12	16/01	01/01
Corby Town	28/10	05/04	09/01		19/12	03/10	24/04	06/02	26/12	29/08	08/08	09/09	20/03	19/08	05/09	02/12	23/01	27/02	24/10	10/04	06/03	14/11
Droylsden	06/02	26/12	05/04	19/09		13/03	27/02	29/08	23/01	09/01	07/09	05/12	28/11	08/08	17/08	24/04	31/10	10/04	05/09	14/11	20/02	17/10
Eastwood Town	19/09	18/08	05/09	20/02	24/10		07/11	09/01	05/04	01/12	05/12	29/08	27/10	26/12	08/08	23/01	10/04	24/04	06/03	08/09	06/02	20/03
Farsley Celtic	28/11	08/08	18/08	31/10	17/04	27/03		08/09	29/08	06/02	26/12	13/03	03/10	05/04	23/01	05/12	14/11	13/02	09/01	05/09	24/10	06/03
Fleetwood Town	15/08	31/10	23/01	12/09	03/04	22/08	01/12		03/10	13/02	24/10	30/01	11/08	10/04	27/02	14/11	13/03	01/01	19/12	24/04	28/12	31/08
Gainsborough Trinity	22/08	13/03	24/04	01/01	15/08	31/08	03/04	20/02		31/10	14/11	10/04	28/12	06/02	19/09	20/03	17/10	12/09	16/01	01/12	19/12	11/08
Gloucester City	31/08	30/01	19/09	03/04	22/08	11/08	15/08	17/10	28/11		27/02	27/10	07/11	24/04	05/12	01/01	28/12	16/01	10/04	20/02	13/03	12/09
Harrogate Town	20/02	17/10	10/04	30/01	27/10	15/08	01/01	20/03	13/02	19/12		07/11	31/08	28/11	24/04	12/09	22/08	03/04	19/09	16/01	11/08	28/12
Hinckley United	28/12	14/11	20/02	16/01	10/08	03/04	12/09	06/03	24/10	20/03	17/04		15/08	19/09	06/02	31/08	01/01	19/12	28/11	31/10	22/08	27/03
Hyde United	13/03	05/09	29/08	17/10	06/03	13/02	19/12	19/09	17/08	07/09	05/04	09/01		23/01	14/11	10/04	24/04	30/11	08/08	26/12	31/10	30/01
Ilkeston Town	03/04	17/04	13/03	28/12	30/01	01/01	31/08	16/01	07/11	03/10	27/03	27/02	22/08		17/10	11/08	01/12	15/08	27/10	13/02	12/09	19/12
Northwich Victoria	19/12	13/02	24/10	07/11	28/12	16/01	11/08	27/10	27/03	17/04	03/10	01/12	12/09	20/02		22/08	15/08	31/08	13/03	30/01	01/01	03/04
Redditch United	07/11	29/08	28/11	27/03	16/01	19/12	17/10	05/09	08/09	26/12	31/10	05/04	06/02	06/03	09/01		20/02	13/03	18/08	08/08	17/04	19/09
Solihull Moors	24/10	19/12	07/11	13/02	27/03	27/02	30/01	08/08	05/09	18/08	09/01	26/12	16/01	08/09	20/03	27/10		03/10	05/04	29/08	28/11	17/04
Southport	23/01	09/01	06/02	28/11	20/03	31/10	19/09	26/12	06/03	08/08	29/08	05/09	17/04	14/11	05/04	24/10	05/12		08/09	18/08	27/03	20/02
Stafford Rangers	01/01	27/02	05/12	11/08	01/12	12/09	22/08	27/03	17/04	14/11	23/01	03/10	20/02	20/03	31/10	28/12	31/08	30/01		17/10	03/04	15/08
Stalybridge Celtic	11/08	27/03	27/10	15/08	12/09	17/04	16/02	07/11	27/02	24/10	06/03	23/01	01/01	05/12	28/11	03/10	03/04	28/12	06/02		31/08	22/08
Vauxhall Motors	24/04	23/01	08/09	05/12	07/11	17/10	10/04	18/08	08/08	05/09	16/02	13/02	27/02	09/01	26/12	30/01	19/09	27/10	29/08	05/04		01/12
Workington	10/04	08/09	26/12	13/03	13/02	28/11	27/10	05/04	05/12	23/01	18/08	08/08	24/10	05/09	29/08	27/02	06/02	07/11	24/04	09/01	03/10	

Please note that the above fixtures may be subject to change.

Football Conference Blue Square South Fixtures 2009/2010 Season	Basingstoke Town	Bath City	Bishop's Stortford	Braintree Town	Bromley	Chelmsford City	Dorchester Town	Dover Athletic	Eastleigh	Hampton & Richmond Borough	Havant & Waterlooville	Lewes	Maidenhead United	Newport County	St. Albans City	Staines Town	Thurrock	Welling United	Weston Super Mare	Weymouth	Woking	Worcester City
Basingstoke Town	■	27/03	12/09	17/04	19/12	15/08	31/08	13/03	01/01	06/02	03/04	06/03	22/08	16/01	07/11	30/01	03/10	28/11	11/08	24/10	08/09	28/12
Bath City	17/10	■	23/01	20/03	31/10	14/11	03/04	06/02	08/09	22/08	28/12	12/09	11/08	05/12	24/04	10/04	06/03	15/08	01/01	20/02	01/12	31/08
Bishop's Stortford	09/01	05/09	■	26/12	01/12	27/10	19/09	27/02	07/11	13/02	17/10	20/03	10/04	08/08	29/08	18/08	05/04	30/01	24/04	14/11	05/12	16/01
Braintree Town	19/09	07/11	01/01	■	20/02	31/08	13/03	13/02	28/11	28/12	22/08	11/08	15/08	24/04	10/04	17/10	27/10	03/04	16/01	05/12	30/01	12/09
Bromley	27/10	17/04	27/03	08/09	■	03/04	22/08	05/12	28/12	15/08	11/08	31/08	16/01	30/01	28/11	13/02	07/11	01/01	12/09	27/02	17/10	13/03
Chelmsford City	23/01	08/08	06/03	05/04	29/08	■	19/12	17/08	06/02	27/03	31/10	07/09	07/11	13/02	05/09	09/01	26/12	17/10	28/11	20/03	03/10	17/04
Dorchester Town	05/04	29/08	20/02	03/10	06/02	10/04	■	31/10	24/10	05/12	08/09	01/12	24/04	18/08	08/08	23/01	09/01	12/09	20/03	26/12	27/02	14/11
Dover Athletic	06/10	19/09	11/08	24/10	20/03	28/12	15/08	■	03/04	12/09	16/01	01/01	20/02	07/11	19/12	24/04	28/11	31/08	22/08	10/04	27/10	30/01
Eastleigh	26/12	13/03	17/04	08/08	18/08	18/08	19/09	27/03	■	27/10	30/01	14/11	17/10	09/01	06/03	05/09	20/02	16/01	05/12	01/12	05/04	31/10
Hampton & Richmond	08/08	28/11	08/09	18/08	23/01	30/01	09/03	09/01	20/03	■	14/11	24/04	31/10	20/02	05/04	26/12	29/08	19/12	10/04	03/10	05/09	17/10
Havant & Waterlooville	29/08	17/08	19/12	23/01	24/10	24/04	07/11	05/09	03/10	19/09	■	13/02	28/11	10/04	09/01	20/03	08/08	26/10	27/02	05/04	26/12	06/02
Lewes	05/09	09/01	24/10	06/02	05/04	20/02	17/04	26/12	19/12	07/11	13/03	■	19/09	28/11	28/10	03/10	19/08	27/03	23/01	08/08	29/08	27/02
Maidenhead United	14/11	13/02	06/02	01/12	03/10	27/02	27/10	08/08	23/01	13/03	17/04	05/12	■	29/08	26/12	05/04	05/09	08/09	24/10	18/08	09/01	27/03
Newport County	31/10	03/10	13/03	27/02	14/11	22/08	28/12	17/04	12/09	12/08	02/12	15/08	03/04	■	23/01	19/12	24/10	06/02	31/08	09/09	27/03	01/01
St. Albans City	01/12	30/01	03/04	14/11	09/03	05/12	16/01	27/03	15/08	31/08	12/09	22/08	01/01	17/10	■	08/09	13/03	28/12	06/02	31/10	17/04	11/08
Staines Town	05/12	24/10	28/12	27/03	19/09	12/09	11/08	01/12	27/02	01/01	15/08	16/01	31/08	27/10	20/02	■	17/04	22/08	07/11	06/02	13/03	03/04
Thurrock	10/04	16/01	31/08	09/03	24/04	01/01	17/10	08/09	22/08	03/04	05/12	28/12	30/01	20/03	13/02	31/10	■	11/08	15/08	12/09	14/11	01/12
Welling United	24/04	27/02	03/10	29/08	26/12	01/12	13/02	05/04	10/04	24/10	06/03	31/10	20/03	05/09	18/08	14/11	23/01	■	19/09	09/01	08/08	05/12
Weston Super Mare	20/02	26/12	31/10	05/09	09/01	13/03	30/01	14/11	13/02	01/12	27/03	17/10	06/03	05/04	03/10	08/08	19/12	17/04	■	29/08	18/08	08/09
Weymouth	13/02	27/10	15/08	19/12	05/09	16/01	01/01	17/10	11/08	17/04	31/08	30/01	28/12	06/03	19/09	28/11	27/03	13/03	03/04	■	07/11	22/08
Woking	20/03	19/12	22/08	31/10	10/04	11/08	28/11	23/01	31/08	16/01	01/01	03/04	12/09	19/09	24/10	06/03	06/02	20/02	28/12	24/04	■	15/08
Worcester City	17/08	05/04	28/11	09/01	08/08	24/10	05/09	03/10	24/04	06/03	20/02	10/04	19/12	26/12	20/03	29/08	19/09	07/11	26/10	23/01	13/02	■

Please note that the above fixtures may be subject to change.

English Football League & F.A. Premier League Tables 1888 - 2009

978-1-86223-184-9

Non-League Football Tables 1889 - 2008

978-1-86223-171-9

Non-League Football Tables 1889 - 2007

978-1-86223-162-7

football league tables & non-league tables

Non-League Football Tables 1889 - 2006

978-1-86223-143-3

AVAILABLE FROM WWW.SUPPORTERSGUIDES.COM

ALL NON LEAGUE FOOTBALL TABLES BOOKS FEATURE THE FOLLOWING LEAGUES :

- Isthmian League
- Football Alliance
- Southern League
- Football Conference
- Northern Premier League

ADDITONAL LEAGUES FEATURED :

 A
- The North West Counties League
- The Manchester League
- The Norfolk & Suffolk League
- The Warwickshire Combination
- The Wessex League
- The Corinthian League
- The Delphian League
- The Midland Alliance
- The Derbyshire Senior League
- The Notts & District League

- The Notts & Derbyshire League
- The Central Alliance

 B
- Hellenic League
- Midland Combination
- Devon County League

 C
- Western League
- South Western League
- Gloucestershire County League

SOCCER BOOKS LIMITED

Supporters' Guides Series

This top-selling series has been published since 1982 and the new editions contain the 2008/2009 Season's results and tables, Directions, Photos, Phone numbers, Parking information, Admission details, Disabled info and much more.

THE SUPPORTERS' GUIDE TO PREMIER & FOOTBALL LEAGUE CLUBS 2010

This 26th edition covers all 92 Premiership and Football League clubs. *Price £6.99*

NON-LEAGUE SUPPORTERS' GUIDE AND YEARBOOK 2010

This 18th edition covers all 68 clubs in Step 1 & Step 2 of Non-League football – the Football Conference National, Conference North and Conference South. *Price £6.99*

THE SUPPORTERS' GUIDE TO SCOTTISH FOOTBALL 2009

The 17th edition featuring all Scottish Premier League, Scottish League and Highland League clubs. *Price £6.99*

THE SUPPORTERS' GUIDE TO NON-LEAGUE FOOTBALL 2007 – STEP 3 CLUBS

Following the reorganisation of Non-League Football the 3rd edition of this book features the 66 clubs which feed into the Football Conference. *Price £6.99*

THE SUPPORTERS' GUIDE TO WELSH FOOTBALL GROUNDS 2007

The 11th edition featuring all League of Wales, Cymru Alliance & Welsh Football League Clubs + results, tables & much more. *Price £6.99*

THE SUPPORTERS' GUIDE TO NORTHERN IRISH FOOTBALL 2007

This 4th edition features all Irish Premier League and Irish Football League Clubs + results, tables & much more. *Price £6.99*

THE SUPPORTERS' GUIDE TO EIRCOM FAI CLUBS 2006

Back after a long absence this 4th edition features all Eircom League Premier and First Division Clubs + 10 years of results, tables & much more. *Price £6.99*

These books are available UK & Surface post free from –

Soccer Books Limited (Dept. SBL)
72 St. Peter's Avenue
Cleethorpes
N.E. Lincolnshire